T0031825

# YOUR BOOK OF
# SHADOWS

# YOUR BOOK OF SHADOWS

## Make your own magical habit tracker

### CERRIDWEN GREENLEAF

CICO BOOKS

LONDON  NEW YORK

Published in 2024 by CICO Books
An imprint of Ryland Peters & Small Ltd
20–21 Jockey's Fields          341 E 116th St
London WC1R 4BW          New York, NY 10029

www.rylandpeters.com

10 9 8 7 6 5 4 3 2 1

Text © Cerridwen Greenleaf 2024
Design © CICO Books 2024
Illustrations © Iratxe López de Munáin
except as otherwise stated on page 144

The author's moral rights have been asserted. All rights reserved.
No part of this publication may be reproduced, stored in a retrieval
system, or transmitted in any form or by any means, electronic,
mechanical, photocopying, or otherwise, without the prior
permission of the publisher.

A CIP catalog record for this book is available from the
Library of Congress and the British Library.

ISBN: 978-1-80065-296-5

Printed in China

Commissioning editor: Kristine Pidkameny
Project editor: Kristy Richardson
Senior designer: Emily Breen
Art director: Sally Powell
Creative director: Leslie Harrington
Production manager: Gordana Simakovic
Publishing manager: Carmel Edmonds

# CONTENTS

# Introduction

Every witch has a set of tools that are vital to the Wicca craft—a besom, an altar, and the many items that adorn it, like incense and candles. One of the most essential tools of all is the Book of Shadows. This book is a sacred space where you can jot down your musings and magical plans, and where you can record the results of your spells.

Like some of the other, more tangible implements in your magical arsenal, your Book of Shadows will help hone and refine your magic. Through my own Book of Shadows, I discovered which moon phases, seasons, and astrological influences render the greatest effect in my spells. By using certain magical correspondences—like crystals, herbs, and candle colors—and noting the results, I came to understand which items produce the best outcome in my

rituals. All the lore, practical know-how, and magical knowledge that I share in this book comes from the detailed notes I keep in my own Book of Shadows.

The following chapters will guide you through all the elements of choosing and using your own Book of Shadows. There are no hard-and-fast rules—your Book of Shadows will be utterly unique, just like you. It is a written expression and documentation of your personal magic workings and should be a book you turn to again and again. Make sure it appeals to you so that you will use it often and well.

## Your Personal Habit Tracker

Your Book of Shadows will become your companion on your Wicca journey. It is a safe space for your musings, sketches, and journaling and will become a book of inspiration, filled with your own thoughts, poetry, and observations. Part journal, part almanac, your Book of Shadows is akin to a personal, magical field guide. At its finest, it should be a history of all your rituals, energy work, circles, spells, and magic you have manifested. It should be a journal of all that you have practiced and wrought.

The records you keep in this sacred tome will aid you in tracking the efficacy of your spells, rites, and charms, enabling you to hone your spellcasting by noting what works best for you. Every ritual is an opportunity to learn and refine your personal magic.

Soon you will have a customized set of "power tools" at your disposal, from favorable moon phases and astrological signs to customized crystals and essential oils, which you can wield for maximum impact in all your workings. Through this process, you will arrive at a highly personalized approach to the craft. Your Book of Shadows will be your guide to increasing your personal power and will help you attain a mastery of witchcraft you never imagined possible.

## Chapter 1

# THE HISTORY AND MYSTERY OF THE BOOK OF SHADOWS

Before you embark on the task of making your own Book of Shadows, let's first begin by exploring the history of these sacred tomes, which have been used by wise women and men for centuries as a practical way to share knowledge of the craft, both within the coven and from generation to generation.

# The Original Book of Shadows

Witchcraft is an ancient tradition, and passing on its wisdom, spells, and lore has informed so much of Paganism through the ages. While this convention has been practiced by witches for centuries, Gerald Gardner—a preeminent forefather of modern witchcraft—was among the first to create a book to be shared and used among his earliest collective, the Bricket Wood Coven.

Gardner described his Book of Shadows as a personal cookbook of spells; his coven could copy the material and add to it as they saw fit. The memorable Doreen Valiente, co-founder and high priestess of the coven, ensured that some of the writing was encoded, or written in a secret text, only to be shared with those who had studied, prepared, and were formally initiated as Wiccans.

Part of the brilliance of these early Wiccans is that they made things easy to understand. Their Book of Shadows simplified magic for many, containing clear instructions for magical rituals and spells, along with a written record of lore and other spiritual writings. This lucidity made witchcraft easier to accept and embrace, and contributed greatly to the popularity of Wicca we enjoy today. It is noteworthy that Gardener's book was one of the first witchcraft documents on record to be openly discussed and broadcast.

Keeping a Book of Shadows soon spread to other covens and Wiccan traditions, such as the Mohsian (an American form of Wicca) and Alexandrian Wicca (founded in the United Kingdom by Alex Sanders in the 1960s). Most importantly, the wisdom became available to individuals, many of whom who were not previously able to practice because they lived in areas and communities where no like-minded folks or covens gathered.

As in the seminal success of the Bricket Wood Coven, the early days of Wicca were largely fashioned around collectives, where a high priest or priestess kept only one Book of Shadows for an entire coven. As Wicca took root and grew in the 1970s, so did the prudence of keeping a Book of Shadows, and it became commonplace for all practitioners to have their own copy. Copies of Gardner's own Book of Shadows, used by his coven, were painstakingly recreated and mailed to other parts of the world. Though originally a secret text only given to initiates of Wicca, many initiates and non-initiates alike have gone on to print various Books of Shadows, and numerous associations have since grown up around this tradition.

Gerald Gardner declared: "a Witch's Book of Shadows is destroyed upon death." Thankfully, that idea was not widely practiced, and these sacred tomes were kept and passed on by very wise elders. Today, we can learn so much from their experiments and findings, gleaned from records kept in these highly informative books.

# The Wiccan Rede

Gerald Gardner did vital work in reclaiming Wicca for the modern era. Gardner and his collective famously formalized the institution of Wicca in the 1970s, when they developed and shared the "bylaws" known as the Wiccan Rede. These bylaws, or redes, provide an excellent guide of conduct for practicing witchcraft—not the "black magic" that led to witches being shunned, punished, and scourged, but magic with positive intentions for the greater good.

# The Golden Rule

Although there are several bylaws, the Wiccan Rede can be summed up with one golden rule: "Do unto others as you would have others do unto you." In other words, the "right" action is up to you and is of paramount importance. You don't have to be Wiccan to appreciate this basic principle. Many people might find it amazing that Neo-Pagans and Christians share this morality, which places personal responsibility at the highest level. This simple guideline is universal in nature—it can apply to any walk of life and to any spiritual practice.

With good intentions, you can learn to become a responsible ritualist. Always consider the short- or long-term effect of your rituals, and how yourself and others will be affected. Careful consideration will go a long way toward increasing the effectiveness of your work.

It is important to recognize that magic is a serious undertaking, which can impact others. Anne Niven, publisher of the excellent *SageWoman*, *PanGaia*, and *newWitch* magazines, recently related an example of a misguided ritual in which young and inexperienced practitioners were advised to invoke an unbalanced spirit to help work through their depression—a potentially dangerous undertaking.

Responsible ritual requires awareness and integrity, traits that will serve you well in every path of your life. To protect yourself, do your research—learn as much as you can about the deities you are invoking. Never take the gods and goddesses lightly, as these ancient energies are very powerful. Honoring the earth and caring for our precious environment is also essential—always carefully consider the herbs, flowers, oils, and essences you intend to use. As a ritualist, you should walk your talk and act responsibly in all your work.

# The Next Generation

Today, millions of people around the world will recognize the Book of Shadows from television shows, like the wildly popular series about three teen witches, *Charmed*, or the cult classic film, *Hocus Pocus*.

While these fictional Book of Shadows may serve to entertain and intrigue viewers, they are unlike those of reality, which don't flip open of their own volition and emit a glow. However, they do introduce the fun of keeping a Book of Shadows—and on that point, I could not agree more. Your Book of Shadows is not a chore but can and should be a labor of love.

Today, a Book of Shadows can take many forms. In Universal Eclectic Wicca (an American tradition that developed in the 1960s), the Book of Shadows is viewed as a personal journal and approached in a free-form way. The coven uses an electronic form, or "ebook of Shadows," which may be shocking to some, but understandable in this modern era. If you are inclined to try a digital path for your Book of Shadows, there are several good apps you can use that will make organization easier, including Microsoft's OneNote or Google Drive—you can even share documents with friends and coven members.

If you like to work on a tablet, laptop, or phone, you can make a digital Book of Shadows. You may prefer to choose and purchase a beautiful journal from a store, which you can decorate and personalize, or even create your own book from scratch. It can be a gorgeous, hand-crafted volume of handmade paper and ribboned bookmarks or a simple three-ring binder. Each Book of Shadows will differ based on the individual composing it. This makes the custom of creating and keeping a Book of Shadows all the more special and all the more beautiful.

# Ancestor Appreciation

Much gratitude is owed to all of those who came before us—from the hedge witches and village healers who suffered persecution in the past, to the Brick Wood Coven of Gerald Gardner, and to those who embraced the reclaimed wisdom of Wicca and ran with it.

The knowledge they have passed down through their Book of Shadows have made it much easier, and more acceptable today, for us to pursue our passions. We are very fortunate indeed for the freedom to practice and enjoy the craft we choose, without fear of inquisition or harsh retribution. We can actively honor our ancestors in a number of ways, including the ritual that is detailed on pages 16–17.

## HONORING WITH OTHERS

Learning about the past is another way to honor our forebears and a group activity, like reading a book or watching a film, would make a wonderful addition to the Ritual of Thanks described overleaf. I belonged to a feminist coven who watched Donna Read's documentary, *Burning Times* (1990) and, while sobering, it was also a way to remember those who passed on their knowledge of the craft.

# Ritual of Thanks

Let us take a moment to give thanks to these brave men and women, whose courage and conviction paved the way for the freedoms we enjoy today. Myrrh and amber are essences that have been used for millennia and are perfect for honoring forebears.

## GATHER TOGETHER

Small table

Representation of one god and one goddess of your choice (such as a statue, a painting, or an icon of a deity you have made)

6 candles (2 yellow, 2 green, and 2 red)

Amber essential oil

Matches

Paper and pen

Fireproof dish

Myrrh incense

Amber incense

Sweetgrass for smudge stick

Choose a table to use for your altar and set out the representations of your chosen deities. Anoint the six candles with the amber essential oil, place them around the table, and light them with the matches. On the paper, write your words of thankfulness to the ancient ones—pass the piece of paper and pen around to all attendees if you are enacting this rite as a group ritual. Now speak this rite:

*Blessed candle, light of the gods and goddesses,*

*I burn this light in gratitude for the witches who came before.*

*Hear my prayer of acknowledgment; hear my prayer of gratitude,*

*Do so with all your grace as we honor all you did for us.*

*We thank you.*

*We honor you.*

*We now walk the path you created.*

*Blessed be thee.*

Read the thank you note(s) aloud. Roll the paper into a scroll and, using a few drops of the warm wax from your candle, seal your sacred statement. Place the paper on your altar. In a fireproof dish, burn the incense and sweetgrass and watch the smoke rise. Those on the other side—your ancestors and forebears—will be drawn to the scented smoke and will be in attendance. Repeat the words of the rite.

This would be a good time for those gathered to express gratitude for those who paved the way for modern witches. It is an excellent time to also discuss future plans for the community, like projects, gatherings, group rituals, or other activities. When the group has shared their wisdom and knowledge, extinguish the flames, and put away the ritual elements. The scroll can be kept and used in Samhain ceremonics (see page 68), when the veil between the living and the dead is particularly thin.

## Chapter 2

# CREATING AND PROTECTING A BOOK OF YOUR OWN

My very first coven was a feminist group of students and collegians. Many of us purchased big, blank binder books from the college bookstore, and used brightly colored pens, pencils, and markers to liberally customize our beginner's Book of Shadows. From this completely blank slate, we recorded our spellwork—making observations and noting essential information on astrological and lunar aspects—and embellished to our heart's content. From these humble beginnings, many beautiful and deeply personal witches' handbooks were born.

# Choosing the Right Book for You

You are going to spend a lot of time with your Book of Shadows, so you should love the look of it. It is up to you to follow your senses when picking out your blank book—what attracts your eye, heart, and mind?

Start by shopping for a blank journal or roomy notebook you find visually appealing. Bookstores, gift stores, and metaphysical five and dimes have lovely options for blank journals, or there are many notebooks with beautiful hardcover bindings and sumptuous sheets of paper. Pick one you simply adore and use that as your Book of Shadows.

There are so many options from which to choose your potential Book of Shadows, you may need a little help while browsing the stores. I suggest taking a pendulum with you—but don't be surprised if it seems to have a mind of its own!

## Show Me Pendulum Spell

Whether your pendulum takes the form of a crystal necklace or a small stone or totem on a cord, it can become an essential tool when vital decisions need to be made.

To use your pendulum, begin by asking, "show me yes" and "show me no." Note the direction the tool swings when it is signaling yes. Then, ask a question for which you know the answer and, again, note the direction of the swing. Now you are ready to use this divination tool.

Narrow down your choice of blank books to the two or three you find most appealing. Holding your pendulum above each in turn, speak this spell:

*Show me the way,*

*Show me true.*

*Which of these books*

*Is the Book of Shadows meant for me?*

*So mote it be!*


After a moment or two your pendulum will indicate a resounding "yes!" and you will have a brand-new Book of Shadows awaiting use in your magic!

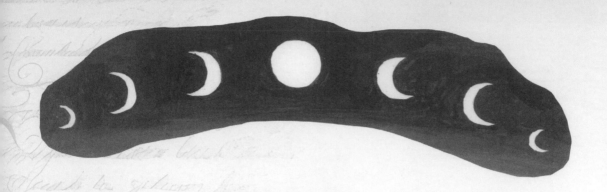

# Claiming Your Book of Shadows

Always be mindful that your Book of Shadows is a magical object and must be treated accordingly. I relish the novelty of every new Book of Shadows and greet each one with great ceremony and expectation.

You will need to place your imprimatur on your Book of Shadows by writing your name on the title page. Witchy colleagues of mine simply write, "The Book of Shadows of [name]" on the front page. You can also include any titles you may hold within your community or coven, such as Priestess.

I like to perform this inscription rite during the New Moon phase to acknowledge the fresh possibilities of this brand-new tool. The New Moon phase (see page 50), which usually lasts three days, is a time to manifest and set new intentions and is the perfect opportunity to inaugurate your new Book of Shadows.

# Inscription Rite

Whether in silver, shiny ink, or in calligraphy letters, inscribe your book in such a way that feels rights to you—make sure it reflects your personality and let the muses move you as you will!

Choose a writing implement and place it on a windowsill for the first night of the New Moon. Arty Pagans may choose an array of brightly colored pens (I have seen many title pages illustrated with colored pens and markers).

On the second morning of the New Moon, open your Book of Shadows to the title page and speak these words:

*Under this Dark Moon,*

*I claim this book as my own.*

*This book is a safe space;*

*This book is a sacred record.*

*With my name, I will claim*

*My rightful tool of magic.*

*This Book of Shadows as mine.*

*And so it is, blessed be!*

Inscribe your name. Leaving your Book of Shadows open at the title page, place it on your altar for another full day and night. Following the third day of the New Moon phase, your sanctified Book of Shadows will be ready to use.

# Make it Personal

Give yourself permission to be wildly creative in your Book of Shadows. Unleash your arty side and decorate the outside of your book with delightful drawings of flowers and herbs, pretty crystals and gems, or starry constellations, moons, and planets in vivid colors. Whatever inspires you is ideal for embellishing the cover and will gladden your heart every time you turn to your Book of Shadows.

Inside the book, use colored pens, inks, and paint (see box, opposite). When I am recording notes about money magic, I use green ink as the color signifies abundance. When I am tracking spellwork in the realm of love, I use red and pink pencils to signify love and romance.

By and large, witches are wildly and wonderfully creative. If you are artistically inclined, as so many witches are, your Book of Shadows is an extraordinary place to draw, design, and doodle. For example, if you are looking for a new home, note down your ideas and draw what you really hope and long for. This helps cement your vision and is a kind of manifesting, as well. By letting your imagination fly, you will intensify and accelerate your magical workings.

By all means, be as imaginative and elaborate as your heart desires—you should love your Book of Shadows and find it pleasing to both your eye and mind.

## COLOR MAGIC

**Pink:** Love, faithfulness, friendship, goodness, and affection.

**Red:** Strength, protection, vitality, sexuality, passion, courage, power, love, and health.

**Orange:** Attraction, stimulation, support, and encouragement.

**Yellow:** Mental ability (especially clear thinking), creative vision, intelligence, study, self-assurance, and prosperity.

**Green:** Money, prosperity, growth, luck, employment, gardening, youth, and beauty.

**Light blue:** Patience, happiness, triumph over adversity, calm, and understanding.

**Dark blue:** Change, flexibility, accessing the unconscious, psychic power, and healing.

**Purple:** Healing, ambition, business success, and power. Alleviates stress.

**Black:** Banishing, absorbing, healing, and attraction (especially money). Alleviates negativity.

**Brown:** Home and garden, animal wisdom, grounding, and healing.

**Gold:** Solar magic, money, attraction, and the astral plane.

**White:** Purification, peace, protection, truth, binding, sincerity, serenity, and happiness.

# Making the Book of Your Dreams

Perhaps the biggest consideration for your Book of Shadows is how to keep it organized. You can follow custom, but you can and should make up your own rules. I urge you to do what feels right for you. Follow your intuition and let that be your North Star. Your inner guidance will never let you down.

## Keeping Notes

I have known Pagans who write their notes and records in a secret code, using other languages, a runic alphabet, or even in high Elvish! While I find this utterly delightful, I make my Book of Shadows easy to use and easy to read.

Many Pagans believe you should write everything by hand in your Book of Shadows, inspired by the belief that this confers personal energy into your work. For me, the charts with astrological information, lunar lore, herbal corresponds, and other practical information need to be perfectly legible. I use my computer for those, carefully glue them onto blank pages of my Book of Shadows, and let them dry.

Keep in mind that as our technology is constantly changing, the way we use it does too. Many people store their Book of Shadows digitally on a flash drive, a laptop, or even virtually. A Book of Shadows accessed through a mobile device or smartphone is no less valid than one inked by hand onto parchment.

## Staying Organized

As you learn more of the craft and your understanding of magic evolves, you will make important connections and want to incorporate additional material in to your Book of Shadows. I have added Pagan prayers, brilliant quotes, and selections from sacred texts that move me to my Book of Shadows.

Some of my more practical friends have chosen a three-ring binder of which they make great use. The beauty of that method is that you can add things so easily; simply snap them in! These pragmatic souls use sheet protectors so their Book of Shadows remain unbesmirched by candle droppings, which can happen when wielding magic.

The more romantic and fanciful of us, including me, prefer a pretty vessel for our magical findings. A binder or book that has a pocket in the back means you can store extra sheets there. If using a binder, you can add them where they best fit your needs. For those who have chosen a blank book, which is bound with a spine, you can add blank pages or preprinted materials, such as tables and lists, through a process called a "tip in" (see below). Crafty witches and DIY bookmakers know this trick, as well.

Whether you go the practical route with a three-ring binder or for a pretty, blank book that is more of an *objet*, your Book of Shadows stores all the information you need for spellcasting and rituals. It is your own personal resource and treasury of lore, which you will utilize often. Those that you share can become part of the collective tradition and be passed down through the ages, and so it is important that the records you keep are clear.

## *Adding Pages*

Tipping-in pages is perfect for those who wish to add extra material to their Book of Shadows, and it is very easy.

### GATHER TOGETHER

Tip-in paper (the material you want to add, such as extra blank pages or printouts)

Scissors

Tape

Start by cutting your tip-in paper to the same size as your Book of Shadows. Allow a little extra space on the edge where you will be securing the page into your book.

Stick the tape to the edge of the tip-in page that will be secured to the book, allowing half the tape to overhang the edge. Take care to trim any surplus tape from the free edges, which will keep the book tidy and avoid problems when sticking the page in.

Open your Book of Shadows to the place where you want to include the tip-in page and line up the edges with the pages inside the book. Press the tape down so that it sticks both the tip-in page and the page that comes before. Using this technique, you can add many pages to the different sections of your Book of Shadows.

# Using Your Book of Shadows with Confidence

Folks that are new to the craft can be intimidated by the very idea of using a Book of Shadows. While this is easy to understand, making a Book of Shadows is a very personal endeavor—let go of that fear of making mistakes. Always remember that perfection can be boring—something that is real and unique is much more appealing and special. Keep an open heart and mind, and your Book of Shadows can become a stunningly beautiful work of art.

## Self-Assurance Charm for Creativity

When one moon ebbs, another grows, and so it goes for our creativity cycles. As the sun sets on a Waxing Moon day (see page 52), you can quiet the voices of inner criticism and banish the creative blocks that get in the way of productivity.

### GATHER TOGETHER

Mortar and pestle

Dried rose petals (1 large or 2 small ones)

2 cinnamon sticks

1 vanilla bean

Sand

Fireproof dish

Charcoal incense disc (available from metaphysical stores)

Fireproof tongs

Matches

Black candle

Peppermint essential oil

In your mortar and pestle, grind together the rose petals, cinnamon sticks, and vanilla bean to a powder.

Add a couple of inches of sand to the bottom of the fireproof dish (for heat insulation) and form a cone shape with the sand (this will allow air to circulate around the charcoal disc). Hold the disc with fireproof tongs, light it with the matches, and place on top of the sand cone. When the charcoal is glowing red and covered with gray ash, you can add a teaspoon of the powder on top of the charcoal.

Anoint the black candle with the peppermint essential oil, and then light the black candle with the matches. Meditate on the flame as the black candle absorbs the negative energy of your inner critic. Allow the positive vibration of the peppermint oil to refresh and uplift your spirits.

As you meditate, think about how you sometimes doubt yourself and your instincts. Visualize working on your new Book of Shadows as you clear self-doubt from your mind. Think about your growing capacity for magic and your potential as you chant:

*Light of the Night Sky,*

*Goddess of the Moon,*

*As you may grow and glow*

*So do my creations,*

*Here, tonight, under your darkling light,*

*I bid goodbye to any doubt.*

*I embrace all within me;*

*All that is right and good,*

*And so it is.*

Blow out the candle, which now contains the energy of your inner critic, and place it outside your home—ideally in the back yard. In the light of the next day, bury the candle in the soil and scatter the dried powders and burnt incense over the top. As you do so, say aloud:

*I bid goodbye to any doubt.*

*I embrace all within me;*

*All that is right and good,*

*And so it is.*

You are now free to create.

# Protecting Your Book of Shadows

Your magical workings and the records thereof are deeply personal.
It makes total sense that you want to keep them private and safe
from curious eyes.

When I first began using a Book of Shadows, I lived in a Queen Anne Victorian
house in the Lower Haight district of San Francisco. It had seen better days, but
my housemates and I could afford the low rent. I didn't think anyone would be
interested in my Book of Shadows, but in those early days of pursuing the craft, I
yearned for a sense of privacy. So, I created a lock for my book of private witchery.

## *DIY Book Lock*

Diary locks have been used for centuries and are easy to make,
perfect for protecting your Book of Shadows.

### GATHER TOGETHER

6 strips of ribbon, each
5in (12.5cm) long

Your Book of Shadows

Hole punch

Scissors

Tape

Small diary lock (available from
hardware or sundry stores)

Braid the strips of ribbon to make a beautiful braid (see box, opposite,
for the ribbon colors that will work well with your zodiac sign).

On the front cover of your book, make a hole close to the outer edge
about halfway down using the hole punch. Repeat on the back cover of
the book, taking care to make sure that the holes align.

Turning to the back of the book, thread one end of the ribbon braid
through the hole. Tie both ends of the braid together and cut off any
excess ribbon. Twist the braid through the hole so that the knot is
closest to the back cover and tape it down.

Turn to the front of the book and bring the braided ribbon loop to
the front cover. Thread the braided loop through the hole inside the cover
and out the front. To lock your notebook, slide the small diary lock into
the loop you have created and secure. Now hide the key!

# LUCKY COLORS OF THE ZODIAC

Choose colors for the ribbons based on your personal sun sign. This will enhance the power of your lock. Below is a quick guide (see also pages 90–93).

**Aries:** Rams are bold and energetic. Their lucky colors are red and orange.

**Taurus:** Taurus folks are practical and steadfast. Their lucky colors are green and pink.

**Gemini:** Twins are flexible and inquisitive. Their lucky color is yellow.

**Cancer:** Those born under the sign of Cancer are nurturing and full of feeling. Their lucky colors are white and silver.

**Leo:** Leos are brave, assured, and charismatic. Their lucky colors are gold and orange.

**Virgo:** Virgos are analytical and pragmatic. Their lucky colors are navy blue and gray.

**Libra:** Libras are balanced charmers. Their lucky colors are pink and light blue.

**Scorpio:** Scorpios are intense and enigmatic. Their lucky colors are black and dark red.

**Sagittarius:** Sagittarians are positive adventurers. Their lucky colors are purple and dark blue.

**Capricorn:** The traits of those born under Capricorn are stability, practicality, and perseverance. Their lucky colors are brown and green.

**Aquarius:** Aquarians are quirky and independent. Their lucky colors electric blue and silver.

**Pisces:** Pisceans are dreamy and imaginative. Their lucky colors are sea green and lavender.

# A Binding Boundary

I have traveled with my Book of Shadows and, while I would never pack mine into a check-in suitcase to be stowed in the hold of a plane, we do have to store book bags, purses and briefcases, or other hand luggage under seats. Extra security measures are needed if carrying your Book of Shadows in this way, and you can protect it with binding magic.

A magic cord is a rope that binds you to an object. This magic cord spell can be useful for anytime you feel the need to guard your Book of Shadows, or if you are looking for an alternative to a lock (see page 30). Simply tie the cord gently around your book and you can rest assured that your spells and rituals will remain safe and sound in your Book of Shadows.

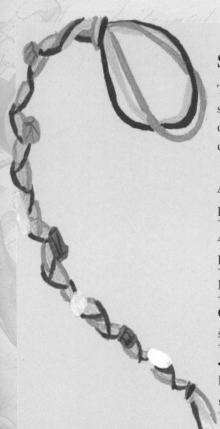

## STONES FOR SAFEKEEPING

To compound the magical quality of your magic cord, adorn it with crystals, stones, and gems by weaving beads into the strands. I recommend using clear quartz crystal beads because they are energy amplifiers. Other meaningful crystals you might want to consider are:

**Amethyst:** Improves intuition and psychic ability.

**Apache tear:** An especially powerful protective stone for women.

**Blue lapis:** Boosts creativity.

**Citrine:** A wonderfully grounding stone that will restore equilibrium.

**Jade:** A shielding stone. Jade is also known to bring prosperity and success in work.

**Lapis lazuli:** Beads strung on gold cord will bring an aura of security.

**Onyx:** A crystal that wards off harm.

**Peridot:** A dark peridot attracts guardian spirits.

**Red coral:** A power stone for security.

**Rose quartz:** Attracts love.

**Tiger's eye:** A safeguarding stone.

# A Safeguarding Spell

The herbs in this spell offer a lot of protection and also clear away negative energies. Palo santo is a pungent and cleansing scent from a tree treasured by shamans as "holy wood" and cedar is widely regarded as a sacred plant in cultures all over the world, where it is used to bless homes. To strengthen the spell, choose one of your lucky colors (see box, page 31) for the braid.

## GATHER TOGETHER

2³/₄yd (2.5m) braid, made from strands of yarn or ribbon

Your Book of Shadows

Small cup of water

Dried cedar smudge bundle

Palo santo smudge bundle

Matches

2 fireproof dishes

Tie your magic cord into a loop at one end to signify feminine energy and leave loose at the other end to represent male energy. Wrap the cord gently around Your Book of Shadows, place it on a table or altar, and set the small cup of water beside it.

Light the cedar bundle with the matches and set it in a fireproof dish to the left of the Book of Shadows. Repeat with the palo santo, which you should place to the right of the book. Allow the sacred smoke to rise and waft over your Book of Shadows. As this happens, say aloud:

*Guardians, Elders, and Spirit Friends,*

*Please keep watch on my Book of Shadows.*

*Let no ill come to my book of me,*

*As I journey on my path of the craft.*

*Imbue me with your knowledge and wisdom*

*As I walk in your footsteps on this chosen path.*

*With blessings and gratitude so mote it be.*

Now place the palo santo on the left and the cedar on the right and repeat the spell.

Quench the burning herbs in the cup of water and stow away the herbs. Before you clean and put away the cup, throw the water from the cup over the threshold in front of your home. By doing this, you will be walking in the path of wisdom of the elders who first used these herbs of protection.

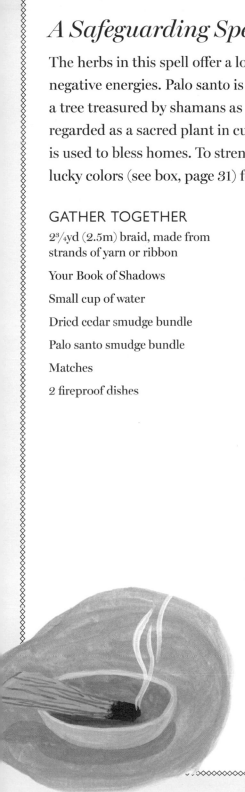

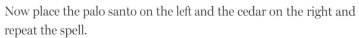

# Protection from the Fairy Realm

Think of the wee ones as your neighbors and allies who have a vested interest in guarding and protecting your home and hearth. Fairies are very territorial of the trees, gardens, and forests they claim as their home—this could be your own back yard or witch's kitchen garden!

Many are fearful of the fey, thanks to age-old legends of mischief. But, after a lifelong fascination with the fairy world, I have delved deeply into this mystical realm and discovered ways to work with them—a thoughtful approach can garner sweet results. Ensure you remain in favor of the fairies, and they will forever remain faithful guardians of you and your sacred Book of Shadows.

# A Garden Sanctuary

When you create a garden sanctuary, it becomes a beacon for fairies. An outdoor space can establish a deep connection to nature, the cosmos, and creation itself. We can lose ourselves in the peace and tranquility of beautiful things and connect with other realms.

It doesn't matter how big your outdoor retreat is. A corner, a porch, a windowsill, or an acre of land can become magnificent and blooming with beauty. If you have a small space, incorporate crystals and mirrors; if you have a large plot of land, have a ball planting a variety of plants, flowers, trees, and shrubs. Place a bench in the middle or add a water feature. Get lost in this refuge of sweet aromas and bursting color and enjoy your slice of heaven on earth.

The Wee Ones love plants. They are attracted to plants that they feel sing to them. The songs come in the form of color, shape, size, and accessibility, which means that the plants should be vibrant, look joyful, smell good, and be close enough to the ground so fairies can dance around them.

Flowering plants that attract butterflies, bees, and birds are what fairies love the most. If you would like to discover other magical floral correspondences, see pages 120–121, or see box (right) for some of the fey favorites.

## FEY FAVORITES

Here are 12 of the best flowering plants that are guaranteed to please fairies and attract them into your garden sanctuary.

Scarlet beebalm or bergamot (*Monarda didyma*)

Common bluebell (*Hyacinthoides non-scripta*)

Fuschia (*Fuchsia magellanica*)

Honeysuckle (*Lonicera*)

Marigold (*Tagetes*)

Nasturtium (*Tropaeolum majus*)

Pansy (*Viola* x *wittrockiana*)

Evening primrose (*Oenothera*)

Foxglove (*Digitalis purpurea*)

Rose (*Rosa*)

Snapdragon (*Antirrhinum majus*)

Wild violet (*Viola odorata*)

# Chapter 3

# THE LABORATORY OF MAGIC

Researchers and scientists keep notes, drawings, records, and observations of their findings in the field. To me, a Book of Shadows has many similarities to a field guide and the spaces where you conduct your magical work are akin to a research site. Like many wise and witchy ones, I am sure you have a special space in your home where you cast spells, perform rituals, and keep your main altar—this is your magical laboratory and I heartily suggest you approach it with a spirit of open-minded experimentation.

# What Works and Why

We all have the highest hope for good results with our spellcasting but, the truth is, not everything will work. Why not? That is the very question you will learn from the records you keep in your Book of Shadows.

Perhaps the moon phase was not ideal. Perhaps the herbs used were not a good match for your magical intention. It is just as important to find out what doesn't work for you as to learn what does. You will refine as you go—every spell is an opportunity, and you will learn something from each potion.

# Intentions for Your Sacred Tool

What are your intentions for your Book of Shadows? Are you recording your rituals to refer to in the future? Are you tracking your results to improve your spellcasting? Would you like to pass your wisdom on to future generations?

Clear intentions for your magic are of paramount importance for successful spellmaking (see page 105). I suggest writing down your intentions and spending some time reflecting upon them. Once you have made and clarified your intentions for your book, you can declare them in much the same way as you would your besom, your athame, crystal ball, wand, and all the other implements in your magical arsenal (see Consecration Charm, opposite). Blessing your book in this way is an important step in imbuing it with an energy of purity and newness.

# Consecration Charm

A Book of Shadows is a distinctly powerful tool. Use this consecration charm to imbue your book with positive intentions.

## GATHER TOGETHER

Small table

Your blank book

Yellow or gold candle

Matches

Smudging sage bundle

Fireproof dish

Arrange a small table in the place where you perform most of your magical workings. Set out the blank book, candle, matches, and the smudging herb bundle in the fireproof dish. Light the candle with the matches and contemplate the flame as it begins to burn.

Next, light the end of the smudging herbs from the candle flame. Walk widdershins (counterclockwise) around the room to cleanse the energy in the space. At the table, cleanse your new blank book by passing it through the purifying sage smoke. You should smudge the interior of the book as well as the outside by passing the blessing herbs over the opening pages.

As the smoke cleanses this new tool, you are charging it with energy and intention. Place the smudging bundle in the fireproof dish and speak this blessing aloud while holding the blank book in both hands:

*By my hand,*

*And this book,*

*And by the blessing of the spirits,*

*The fire of my mind and heart*

*Will create much magic*

*For the betterment of the world.*

*This sacred tool abets my craft.*

*And so it is.*

Lay the book back on the table and leave it open. Extinguish the candle and the smudge stick and put them away with the other elements. Leave your new Book of Shadows out for a full day and night.

# A Shrine for Your Book of Shadows

**It is important to remember that a Book of Shadows is a singular item—a tool all in and of itself—and should not be casually placed where the vibrations of other magical items can have an effect.**

I keep my Book of Shadows on a tiny altar dedicated to that purpose. I use a small three-legged stool, which is the perfect size. I drape a beautiful cloth over it, which is currently a deep purple with golden threads shot through, which offers my Book of Shadows a perfect perch. You can use whatever works for you—a small table can suffice, if it befits your Book of Shadows and will maintain its integrity.

I don't keep candles, incense, or crystals on this shrine, so that the energies of these elements do not intermingle and cause an undue influence on the Book of Shadows. I carry out spells on my main altar so that, similarly, the energies are not intermingled with the energy of this deeply sacred book.

It is essential to regard your Book of Shadows with the respect you would any other magic tools. I have known a couple of witchy acquaintances who left their Books of Shadows lying around at home—not just where they performed magical workings, but also in the kitchen where they became a bit tattered and stained. I was not surprised when they later remarked that they weren't finding their Book of Shadows to be as effective as they hoped. It was the aforementioned mixing of energies that got in the way of the success in spells. By bearing that in mind, you will have much greater results.

# Shrine Blessing Ritual

Blessing the shrine where you keep your Book of Shadows is highly recommended and you can do that best by clearing space and cleaning.

## GATHER TOGETHER

Cup of freshly drawn water

Large white bowl

Your shrine (a stool or small table)

¼ cup of salt

Small white bowl

Clean and dry white cloth

Black candle

Matches

Smudging herb bundle
(see pages 122–123 for
purifying herbs)

Fireproof dish

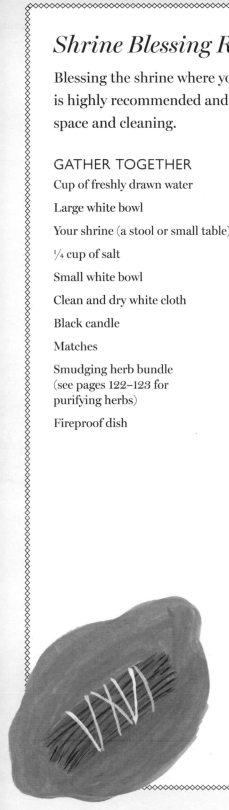

Start by placing a cup of freshly drawn water in a large white bowl beside the shrine. Pour salt into the small white bowl until it is filled halfway and leave on top of the shrine overnight.

In the morning, dip a corner of the cloth into the water. Gently rub the surface of the shrine with the damp cloth. Let it dry naturally and do the same with the floor where the shrine will be placed. Next, throw the salt out of the front door into the sidewalk or street and then throw the water in the same direction.

Place the black candle in the large white bowl and light it with the matches. Using the candle flame, light the smudging herb bundle. Speak the following spell aloud:

*Clean and clear,*

*New magic will be made here.*

*Blessed by the elements,*

*Knowledge will be enshrined here,*

*So mote it be.*

Walk around the space with the smudging herb bundle until the room is infused and imbued with the scent and purification of the sacred smoke. Repeat the spell once again and then extinguish the smudging bundle and the candle. Remove the bowls, candle, fireproof dish, and smudging herbs from the room. Wash the cloth by hand and let it dry and be purified by the sun.

The newly cleansed stool or table is now ready to be positioned in the place where you want to keep your shrine.

# A Table of Contents

The table of contents is the structure upon which an entire book—even your Book of Shadows—hangs. It is an excellent foundation to guide you on the highest path of witchery.

I recommend the following approach as shown to me in my early days of the craft. Blessedly, these elements are nearly always universally included as they are important aspects of any Book of Shadows.

## Laws of Your Coven or Tradition

Magic has rules. While traditions and rubrics vary, the laws are—put simply—guidelines that ensure magic is performed for good. Even if you're part of an eclectic tradition that doesn't have written rules, or if you're a solitary witch, the front of your book is a good place to write down what you think are acceptable rules of magic. This may include the Wiccan Rede (see page 12) or an alternative your coven has adopted.

## Dedication

A dedication is a good place to state who you are dedicating yourself to and why. Initiated witches may wish to include the words of their initiation ceremony in their Book of Shadows. Alternatively—and a wonderful way to go for solo practitioners—it is to devote your Book of Shadows to a deity for which you feel a deep affinity (see page 137 for a list of deities and their domains). While I have been initiated, I choose to dedicate to my goddess of choice, as this example:

*I, Cerridwen, dedicate myself to The Mother of us all,*

*The great Goddess Gaia today, June 21st, 2024.*

*On this Midsummer Day and every day for as long as I shall live,*

*I dedicate my magical workings to our planet,*

*To our Mother Earth and our collective future.*

# Correspondence Tables

When I was first learning the ways of witchery, in the early stages of understanding correspondences and connections, I found this aspect of the Book of Shadows to be the most important of all. In the art of spellcasting, correspondence tables (see pages 116–137) are among your most essential tools.

Metals, stones and crystals, colors, essential oils, animals, and numbers all have different significance and purpose. Trees, flowers, plants, and herbs also have their own magical qualities. Herbalism is often considered the core of spellcasting because plants are an ingredient that people have used for thousands of years. Ask an experienced Pagan or Wiccan about any herb, and chances are that they'll expound not only on the magical use of the plant, but also on its healing properties and its history of use. Keeping a chart of some sort in your Book of Shadows guarantees that this information will be at the ready when you really need it. (Remember, many herbs should not be ingested, so it's important to research thoroughly.)

Deities also influence our lives in so many ways and it is useful to keep a list of gods, goddesses, and spirits, and their spheres of influence, in your Book of Shadows. Honoring these benevolent beings is vital, and your book is also a good place to keep stories and artworks of the legends and myths concerning your deity. If your practice is an eclectic blend of different spiritual paths, you can include that too—there is a wealth of pantheons, and it is an excellent idea to be inclusive and learn from other traditions as your magical understanding evolves.

## Calenders and Almanacs

If you have access to a good almanac, it's a good idea to record a years' worth of moon phases in your Book of Shadows. Charts showing the movement of the sun, stars, and planets can be useful too. As you track the changing seasons, gather information about herbs, flowers, and trees, and their uses throughout the year.

## High Holidays, Sabbats, Esbats, and Other Rituals

The Wheel of the Year (see page 66) includes eight holidays for most Wiccans and Pagans, although some traditions do not celebrate all of them. Your Book of Shadows can include rituals for each of the Sabbats. For Samhain, you may wish to create a rite to honor your ancestors or at Beltane you may wish to gather with family and friends.

If you celebrate each Full Moon (see pages 114–115), you may include an Esbat rite in your Book of Shadows. You can use the same one each month, or create several different ones tailored to the time of year. If you perform any Full-Moon rites for healing, prosperity, protection, or other purposes, you can record them here.

## Spellcasting and Divination

When you experiment with a new spell or charm, or new methods of divination—like Tarot, scrying, or astrology—keep a record of what you do and the results you see in your Book of Shadows. Noting the phase of the moon, the day of the week, the elements you use in the ritual (and their color, number, and so on), will all have an effect on your magical workings.

# Sacred Texts, Magical Recipes, and Indices

While it's fun to have a bunch of new shiny books on Wicca and Paganism to read, sometimes it's just as nice to have information that's a little more established. If there is a certain text that appeals to you, such as The Charge of the Goddess (an old prayer in an archaic language), or a particular chant that moves you, include it in your Book of Shadows.

As you discover recipes for oils, incense, or herb blends, keep them in your Book of Shadows. You may even want to include a section of food recipes for Sabbat celebrations. There's a lot to be said for "kitchen witchery." For many, the kitchen is the center of hearth and home.

If you find a rite, spell, or interesting piece of information, be sure to note down the source. You may also want to keep notes about books you've read and what you thought of them. This way, when you get a chance to share information with others, it will help you to keep things straight and you'll start to recognize patterns in authors' works. You may want to use one notebook for information copied from books or downloaded off the Internet, and another for original creations. Find the method that works best for you, and take good care of your Book of Shadows. After all, it's a sacred object and should be treated accordingly.

## Chapter 4

# TRACKING LUNAR EFFECTS IN YOUR SPELLCASTING

Do you gaze up at the night sky in wonder? I know I do, nearly every night. Since prehistory, we have looked toward the moon for inspiration from the divine. The moon is both magical and majestic, mysterious and reflective. She rules the ocean tides, the crops in our fields, and our moods and emotions, and is one of the most important lights in our sky. Let Luna be your guide as you design and develop your own moon ceremonies and rites of the night.

# Moon Spell Magic

If I had to choose only one kind of magic to do, I would choose lunar rites, or what I call "moon spell magic." The possibilities are endless when you are working with lunar enchantments since the different moon phases each have distinct magic properties.

A good practice is to cast the same spell throughout the lunar cycle, taking note of the moon phase. Measure the effect and add the results to your Book of Shadows. Over a few months, you will come to know the best times for your spellwork.

## The Phases of the Moon

Each lunar cycle begins with a New Moon phase. This takes place when the moon lies between the sun and the Earth so its illuminated side cannot be seen from the Earth. The moon gradually waxes (grows), moving to the opposite side of the Earth and, when it has reached the far side, its illuminated side faces us as the Full Moon. As it completes its orbit around the planet, it wanes until it apparently vanishes. The entire cycle, during which the moon orbits the earth, takes approximately a month.

Performing a ritual at the optimal time of the lunar cycle will maximize your power. Each moon phase has a distinct energy that is conducive to certain spells. The New Moon, or Dark Moon, is the beginning of the cycle and is excellent for setting intention and starting new endeavors. The Waxing Moon is "growing" and, therefore, best for matters of abundance. Matching your magical intention to the moon phase is a really smart move.

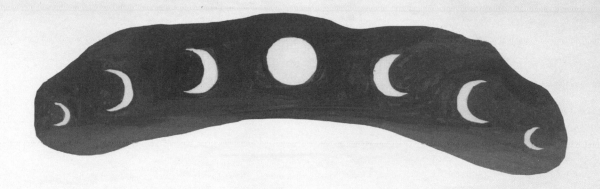

## Timing Your Rituals with Astrology

Incorporating your own astrological chart will help refine your spellwork enormously. The moon moves into a new sign every two to three days, and knowing when the moon aligns with your sign is essential (see also pages 100–101). To determine the sun sign governing the moon on any given day, you will need a celestial guide or almanac (there are wonderful options online, such as www.cafeastrology.com).

Through this enjoyable and inspiring process, I know that the moon in Scorpio is a powerful time for me to perform rites about love and romance, and that the moon in Pisces is also a fruitful time. Your magic is singular to you. By paying attention to the movements of the moon and stars in the sky, you can customize your craft to what works best for you.

In addition to the personal power of your own sun sign, there are multitudinous associations with the moon that can work in your favor, from colors and crystals to deities and days of the week. The more corresponding energies you can weave in to your spellwork, the better the outcome. See the correspondence charts on the following pages (and on pages 116–137) to align your magical intentions.

# New Moon

Also known as the Dark Moon, the New Moon is a time to begin new projects and bring new energy into your life—budding and building are the key words for the New Moon.

This phase is a wonderful opportunity to involve yourself in personal improvement and transformation, whether spiritual or health-related, from practicing yoga to following a new diet. I also try to start new ventures during this phase—it's the perfect time to plant a garden, reorganize an office, start a new business, begin an art project, or embark on a new relationship ... anything that requires energy for developing and growing. The New Moon also has great advantages for healing.

Rituals and charms commenced in the New Moon tend to have tangible results by the next New Moon.

## DIANA'S BOW

The New Moon is sometimes called Diana's Bow, a reference to the Roman goddess of the hunt. This maiden phase arrives when the moon begins to show its first glimmering crescent of light, reminiscent of the goddess's favored weapon. You can call upon Diana during your magical workings and ask her to bestow favor on your new projects.

MAGICAL CORRESPONDENCES
## ... for New Beginnings

**Days:** Monday and Sunday.

**Colors:** Black, dark blue, and deep purple.

**Herbs:** Chamomile, mugwort, yarrow, lavender, agrimony, and passionflower.

**Incense:** Myrrh, cinnamon, basil, rose, ginger, and lavender.

**Essential Oils:** Roman chamomile and lavender.

**Crystals:** Labrodrite, black tourmaline, lapis lazuli, obsidian, and smoky quartz.

**Metal:** Silver.

# Incantation for New Ideas

The first night of the New Moon is the best time to sow the seeds for the things you want to bring into your life and your future. Fresh ideas, innovation, and inspiration will be yours with this Dark Moon magic.

## GATHER TOGETHER

Purple cloth

3 purple candles

Smudging bundle of dried lavender blooms

Fireproof dish

Matches

Lavender essential oil

Pick a spot outside—your back yard, deck, or somewhere outside your home is perfect for this rite. Lay the purple cloth on the ground and set the purple candles on this "mobile altar." Set down the smudging bundle in a fireproof dish and light with the matches.

Using the matches, scratch your name into the first candle. Scratch your hope into the second candle (with as much brevity as possible—"new ideas" or "artistic vision" will work well, as long as it is true to your intention). On the third candle, inscribe a circle representing the energy of the Dark Moon. Anoint the three candles with essential oil.

Light your name candle with the matches and recite:
*This candle burns for me.*

Light the candle of hope and say:
*Here burns my hope for* [your intention].

Light the candle of inspiration and say:
*Here burns the flame of my mind, alight and alive with new ideas.*

With your eyes closed, picture yourself enacting your hope and desire. Picture yourself in the company of a person who inspires you and imagine them walking beside you, encouraging you to achieve your goal. After a few minutes, extinguish the candles and smudging bundle in the fireproof dish. Place all the ritual elements on your main altar inside the house for the remaining three days of the Dark Moon phase.

Get ready for an abundance of inspiration and inventive ideas to come your way. Be sure to record the results in your Book of Shadows!

# Waxing Moon

As the moon grows full and abundant during this phase, rituals and invocations for positive change will come to fruition. Ceremonies for luck, growth, and love will succeed during the Waxing Moon.

## Love and Romance

The moon is in full maiden aspect for the fourteen days of the typical waxing period (for more information about the maiden, see The Triple Goddess on page 70). The Waxing Moon is a time for relationships to flourish. If you are fortunate enough to have a soul mate, or if there is someone you would like to get to know better, the Waxing Moon is the perfect phase to seal your fate together. Power up this lunar influence with other correspondences (see box, below) to ensure that you are lucky in love. Friday, for example, is associated with Venus and its ruling goddess of love.

## MAGICAL CORRESPONDENCES
### ...for Love

**Day:** Friday.

**Colors:** Pink and red.

**Herbs:** Aster, beet, bleeding heart, cardamom, chestnut, chickweed, elm, lovage, pear, pimento, plumeria, and rose.

**Incense:** Amber, gardenia, hibiscus, jasmine, orange, rose, and strawberry.

**Essential Oils:** Carnation, dragon's blood, ginger, jasmine, myrtle, rose, and ylang ylang.

**Crystals**: Blue topaz, chryscholla, garnet, jade, rose quartz, rhodochrosite, serpentine, and tourmaline.

**Metal:** Nickel.

# Soul Mate Sorcery

Invite your loved one or the object of your desire over on a Friday night, the night of Waxing Moon romance. The pink candle will bring sweetness and the red candle will bring deep affection to the evening.

## GATHER TOGETHER

2 long-stemmed roses in a vase

2 candles (pink and red)

Rose essential oil

Ylang ylang essential oil

Matches

Amber incense

Fireproof dish

Chilled pink Champagne

2 ripe strawberries

2 Champagne flutes
(gold will work best)

Using a thorn from your rose, scratch your intentions for the evening into the candles—for example, love, romance, marriage, or anything that feels true for you and your relationship. Anoint the candles with the essential oils. With the matches, light the candles and the amber incense—a truly seductive scent—in the fireproof dish.

Give the object of your affection one of the roses and keep the other for yourself. As you bestow the flowers, speak the following aloud:

*Friend so dear,*

*Friend so near,*

*With open hearts and minds.*

*We come together, ever closer.*

*With trust and true affection,*

*Our bond is true, together forever,*

*Our souls mate in joy and bless,*

*So mote it be. Blessed be!*

Ask your dear one to uncork the Champagne while you add the ripe strawberries to the bottom of the Champagne flutes. Fill the glasses and toast your new intimacy. When you have sipped all the Champagne, feed each other the infused strawberries. Extinguish the candles and incense and see what happens next!

## Prosperity and Plenty

The Waxing Moon is a fortuitous time for manifesting magic and, as the moon burgeons during this phase, tap into its power to bring forth abundance and prosperity.

Thursdays are considered a day of luck and plenty and, along with other magical correspondences (see box below), you can incorporate Thursday's divine influence into your money magic for that extra heavenly boost. Thursdays are named for the powerful Norse god, Thor, and I often refer to this day as "Thor's day." Thursdays are also ruled by Jupiter, who stands for joviality, expansion, and all things abundant. I was born on a Thursday, too, which makes me feel like it is even more of a day of good fortune for me.

### MAGICAL CORRESPONDENCES
## ... for Money

**Day:** Thursday.

**Color:** Green.

**Herbs:** Almond, bergamot, ginger, golden seal, nasturtium, moonwort, moss, oakmoss, grapes, and sarsaparilla.

**Incense:** Basil, bergamot, jasmine, oakmoss, orange, patchouli, and vetiver.

**Essential Oils:** Lemongrass, cinnamon, sandalwood, bergamot, and eucalyptus.

**Crystals:** Aventurine, blue topaz, jade, and serpentine.

**Metals:** Silver and copper.

## Abundance Charm

The nasturtiums used in this spell bloom in cheery yellow, red, and orange hues that embody the spirit of providence. Offer these blooms to a magnanimous god or goddess to attract their generosity. Performing this spell early on a Thursday during a Waxing Moon phase will bring excellent financial opportunities your way.

### GATHER TOGETHER

1 green candle

1 gold candle

Bergamot essential oil

Matches

Jasmine incense

Fireproof dish

Jade crystals in various shades of green

Green bowl

Small cup of water

Bunch of fresh nasturtium flowers

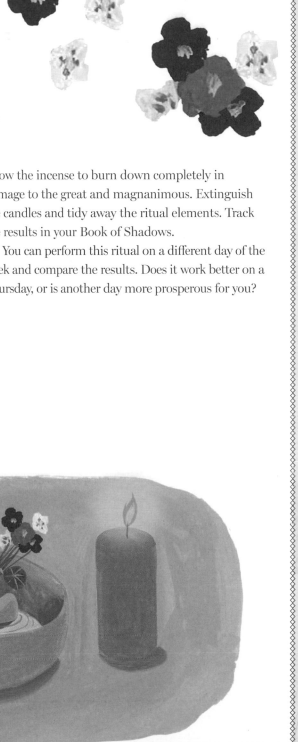

Place the candles on your altar and anoint them with the essential oil. Light the candles with the matches and take a moment to breathe in the uplifting scent. Light the incense with the matches and place in the fireproof dish.

Place the jade crystals in the green bowl and fill with a little water from the cup. Place the bowl between the two candles and add the bunch of nasturtium flowers. Standing in front of the altar, with arms outspread, speak the following aloud:

*Under this sun and moon of increase.*

*All is well, all is at peace.*

*The wisdom of the gods will never cease,*

*I ask of you on this day to please release*

*For the grace of abundance for me to increase,*

*Gratitude and love to you always—so mote it be!*

Allow the incense to burn down completely in homage to the great and magnanimous. Extinguish the candles and tidy away the ritual elements. Track the results in your Book of Shadows.

You can perform this ritual on a different day of the week and compare the results. Does it work better on a Thursday, or is another day more prosperous for you?

# Full Moon

When the moon is full, Mother Moon is at her zenith, parading in all her glory across the night sky. The Full Moon is pure power—her luminous glow surrounds us and promotes strength and supremacy.

Rituals during this phase can be transformative, calling forth your personal power. Take time, also, to honor lunar deities during this phase. The best way to acknowledge their influence and importance in our lives is to honor them outside, under a moon-lit night sky. Whether you are performing solo spells or taking part in a group ritual, always speak the names of lunar goddesses aloud in gratitude. Using candles or a bonfire during these magical workings will reflect and enhance the light of our lunar queens of the night.

The Full Moon also enhances psychic awareness, so cleanse your scrying mirrors, tarot decks, and crystals. The Full Moon is a time for prophecy and divinatory rituals performed during this time can bring great clarity.

## MAGICAL CORRESPONDENCES
### ... for Creativity

**Days:** Sunday and Wednesday.

**Colors:** Orange and yellow.

**Herbs:** Angelica, basil, coltsfoot, crocus, rosemary, hemp, and kava kava.

**Incense:** Cinnamon and peppermint.

**Essential Oils:** Cinnamon, lavender, and rosemary.

**Crystals:** Agate, aventurine, blue lace agate, carnelian, kunzite, lapis lazuli, opal, and topaz.

**Metals:** Gold and copper.

# Once in a Blue Moon

"Once in a Blue Moon" refers to rare and special occasions. How do we know when the Blue Moon occurs? It is on that remarkable instance when two Full Moons occur in one calendar month to give us an "extra," or thirteenth, Full Moon of the year.

Every witch is a soulful person and the Blue Moon is an occasion for deep spellcasting for these true spiritual seekers. Try the Spritual Heights Spell (see pages 58–59) to tap into the transformational magic of this special celestial moment and reach your full spiritual potential.

The Blue Moon is to be used wisely. Take this opportunity to consider long-term plans and goals and to give thanks for what you have accomplished. As you take stock, be grateful for what you have and for the people in your life—good health, children, a job you enjoy, good friends, a comfortable home, and all the opportunities before you. All Blue Moon rituals should contain an aspect of thanksgiving, to the gods and goddesses and to Mother Nature, who gave you life.

# Spiritual Heights Spell

Many Pagans believe the Full Moon to be the phase with the most potent power. If so, the rare, second Full Moon in a month will have the most extraordinary strength of all. The two copper pennies represent both the Full Moons of this month. Perform this spell outside at twilight on the first night of the Blue Moon to bring new understanding into your life and perhaps, even an epiphany or two.

## GATHER TOGETHER

Yellow scarf or cloth

Outdoor altar, small table, or three-legged stool

1 large yellow candle

Rosemary essential oil

2 copper pennies

Round, blue dish

Matches

Cinnamon incense

Fireproof dish

Clean and dry yellow sheet (like a bedsheet or other material)

Paper and pen

Place the yellow cloth over your outdoor altar. Anoint the large yellow candle with the essential oil and place it in the middle of the altar. Place the two copper pennies in the dish and place the dish in front of the candle. Light the candle with the matches and then light the cinnamon incense from the candle and place in the fireproof dish. Unfold the yellow sheet and spread it in front of the altar. With your pen and paper, lay down on the sheet where you can see the bright, beautiful Blue Moon above you. Speak aloud:

*Sister Moon who shines so bright*

*Tonight, I take shelter under your light.*

*I feel love and healing from you this night.*

*Please shower upon me your wisdom and insight.*

*Please teach me all that is good and right.*

*I thank you for these mysteries I will write.*

*Blessed be thee; so mote it be.*

Gaze at the moon above and take in its rare glory. As you appreciate your surroundings and reflect on your blessings, relax and enjoy the respite. Allow insights to flow down to you. As new ideas and inspiration begin to flow—and they will—note them down. Take your time and don't rush as this may block the blessings.

When you are ready, rise, and extinguish the candle and incense. Pack up the ritual elements but leave the two pennies outside. Tuck them away in a place where they are "hidden in plain sight," and can absorb and reflect the light of every Full Moon.

Transfer your notes to your Book of Shadows. Make sure you look back and reflect on them at every Full Moon. New insight and understanding will continue to come, long after this ritual has been completed.

# Waning Moon

The moon has reached her zenith and now begins her journey home, completing her orbit around the Earth. As she returns, her energy ebbs and she begins to wane and grow smaller. This phase, for us too, is a time to conserve our power, to turn our attention toward home and inner peace and wisdom.

## Creating a Sanctuary

Spellcasting during the Waning Moon phase should be concerned with conserving energy, creating a peaceful sanctuary full of positivity, so you can rest and replenish. The home is a sanctuary, a sacred space that protects you and your loved ones. Anyone, especially the highly sensitive or psychic, will pick up on lingering vibrations, so it is important to keep your space fresh, healthy, and free of negative energies and chemicals. Whether you are moving into a new home, have frequent visitors, or simply need to rest and replenish, it is of vital importance to clear out old, stale, and possibly negative energies from your domain.

**MAGICAL CORRESPONDENCES**

## ...for Protection

**Days:** Tuesday, Wednesday, Thursday, Friday, and Saturday.

**Colors:** Black, blue, purple, red, and white.

**Herbs:** Anise, bay laurel, blueberry, chives, chrysanthemum, dogwood, lemon, rose, and snapdragon.

**Incense:** Anise star, clove, grapefruit, pine, lavender, and willow.

**Essential Oils:** Amber, angelica, carnation, cedarwood, eucalyptus, hyacinth, and rose geranium.

**Crystals:** Black jasper, blue lace agate, desert rose, goldstone, red jasper, and tanzanite.

**Metals:** Bronze, iron, lead, steel, and titanium.

# Spiritual Scrub

Banish old energies from your sacred space with this cleansing ritual. Performed on a night of a Waning Moon cycle, it is a powerful way to cleanse and protect your home … and the smell of a room freshly cleaned with lemons and natural, scented oils feels wonderful.

## GATHER TOGETHER

1 cup hot water

5 quart (4l) glass mixing bowl

8 drops pine essential oil

6 drops lavender essential oil

6 drops peppermint essential oil

Juice of 8 lemons

3 juniper berries

3 cinnamon sticks

Wooden spoon

2 gallon (7.5l) utility bucket

Freshly drawn hot water (to three-quarter fill the bucket)

1 quart (1l) white vinegar

Kitchen sieve

Clean towel

New mop

Pour the cup of hot water into the bowl and add the essential oils, lemon juice, juniper berries, and cinnamon sticks. Stir this mixture widdershins (counterclockwise) with a wooden spoon and leave to steep. After half an hour, fill the bucket with the hot water and add the white vinegar. Using a sieve, strain the herbal mix from the bowl into the bucket and stir three times widdershins with the spoon.

Dip the towel into the mixture and use it to clean all the doorhandles in your home. The doorknobs of your front door and back door are extremely important, but I recommend you clean throughout your home, including drawer pulls, appliance handles like refrigerator door handles, and any other handles that are frequently touched. Before you launder the towel, take it outside and let it dry in the sun.

Now, wash the floors with the mop. As you mop, speak this spell:

*My home is my temple,*

*and here I will live and love.*

*Here, I will work and learn,*

*Here, I will share food and be healed.*

*And so it is by magic sealed.*

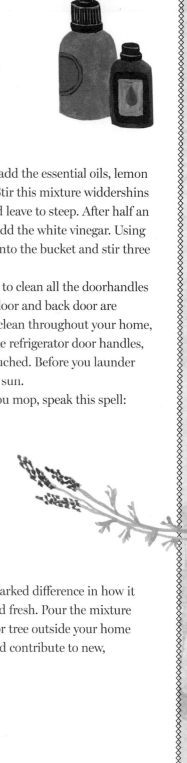

Once the space is cleansed, you will note a marked difference in how it feels. It will be utterly natural, light, clear, and fresh. Pour the mixture from the bucket on the base of a large bush or tree outside your home where it can become part of a living thing and contribute to new, positive growth.

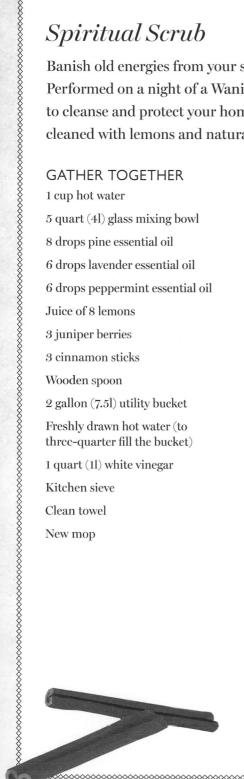

# Finding Peace

A peaceful life is a happy life. A state of peacefulness in your own heart can help instill more of that hopeful and positive energy into the world. Try this simple spell (shown right) to bring a sense of calm and harmony into your life, so you can rest and replenish during this Waning Moon phase.

## MAGICAL CORRESPONDENCES
## ... *for Peace*

**Day:** Monday.

**Colors:** Blue, pink, and white.

**Herbs:** Chamomile, gardenia, lavender, lily of the valley, myrtle, passionflower, tuberose, vervain, and violet.

**Incense:** Chamomile, gardenia, lavender, lilac, and sandalwood.

**Essential Oils:** Almond, chamomile, gardenia, lavender, sandalwood, and violet.

**Crystals:** Pink quartz, celestite, chryscholla, kunzite, lepidolite, rhodochrosite, and selenite.

**Metal:** Copper.

# *Rose Water Blessing Bowl*

Three simple ingredients—a pink candle, a white gardenia, and water—can bestow a powerful calming influence. The gardenia signifies beauty, peace, and love, which can blossom to encompass yourself, others, and the Earth. The candle represents the flame of the East, the light of the soul that brings unity, harmony, and higher intentions. Water is the element of the West that, like our emotions, is cleansing and free-flowing.

## GATHER TOGETHER
Rose quartz

Bowl of freshly drawn water

A white gardenia

Pink candle

Matches

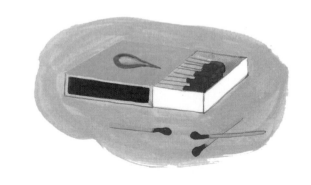

Place the rose quartz at the bottom of the bowl of water and float the gardenia on top. Now, light a pink candle with the matches. With the fingers of your left hand, gently stir the water, and speak the blessing:

*I give myself life and health, refreshing water for my spirit.*

*I give myself time to rest, and space to grow.*

*I am love. My heart is as big as the world.*

*I have peace of mind and intend that for everyone,*

*May the world know the gentle power of peacefulness,*

*So be it, now and always.*

Take some time to meditate—visualize yourself filling with inner peace, and feel it spreading out into the world. Contemplate what a more peaceful world would look like. Once you feel a sense of calm and optimism, blow out the candle and store it away.

Place the water with the gardenia and quartz on your altar for two days. Every time you smell the rich, sweet scent of gardenia infusing the room, imagine peace infusing the world.

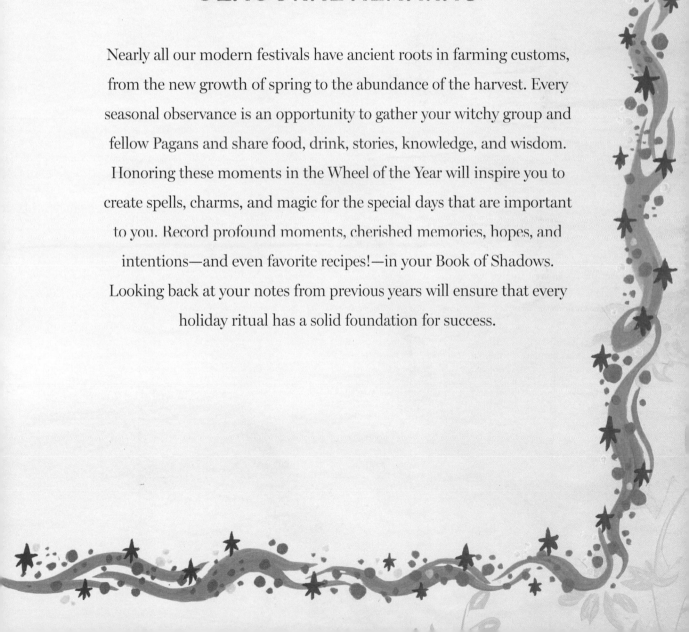

# Chapter 5

# FINDING INSPIRATION IN THE SEASONAL ALMANAC

Nearly all our modern festivals have ancient roots in farming customs, from the new growth of spring to the abundance of the harvest. Every seasonal observance is an opportunity to gather your witchy group and fellow Pagans and share food, drink, stories, knowledge, and wisdom. Honoring these moments in the Wheel of the Year will inspire you to create spells, charms, and magic for the special days that are important to you. Record profound moments, cherished memories, hopes, and intentions—and even favorite recipes!—in your Book of Shadows. Looking back at your notes from previous years will ensure that every holiday ritual has a solid foundation for success.

# The Wheel of the Year

The Pagan Wheel of the Year turns on the holidays, each one a seasonal highlight for Pagans. They are a time to share sacred rites, good food and drink, and to revel in the joy of being in a community.

The Samhain festival (October 31–November 1) marks the beginning of the Pagan year. As a Pagan, I am both charmed and amused that, in recent years, Halloween has become the second biggest consumer holiday in North America. These seasonal observances are an opportunity for everybody, from all walks of life, to feast, celebrate, and create important and meaningful memories.

Traditionally, holidays were created to observe the changing of the seasons. In the Northern Hemisphere, Samhain marks the autumn equinox—the end of the harvest season and the beginning of winter. Others, such as Imbolc (traditionally held on February 1) and Beltane (May 1) celebrate springtime and new growth, while Lughnasadh marks the beginning of the harvest season and Yule marks the winter solstice (around December 21), during the dark and chilly days of midwinter.

In my Book of Shadows, the pages that delve into the seasons—and their associations and traditions—contain more notes and records than any other section. This may well be the same for you! As a child, you doubtless felt an affinity for certain flowers or animals. Your natural attraction to these plants and creatures may be astrologically ordained and uncovering your own unique astrological connection to nature will inform your spellcasting for decades to come. I have always loved weeping willow trees, even as a tiny toddler. Their flowing branches and rich green leaves are so beautiful, and their poetic appearance is soothing to my spirit. Once I began studying astrology, I learned that my Pisces moon is deeply drawn to this watery and wonderful tree—it inspires my dreamy Piscean imagination and romanticism. What are the trees, herbs, plants, and flowers that speak to you? List them, draw the flowers and plants, or take snapshots and paste them into your Book of Shadows.

# Samhain (Hallows)

Samhain, also known as Hallows or All Hallow's Eve, is the celebration of the Celtic New Year, and perhaps the modern Pagan's favorite high holiday of all.

Samhain marks the turning of the great wheel—a time to honor and commune with those who have passed on to the other side, as well as a time to celebrate the passing year and set intentions for the coming one. Plus, it is the season to become your most bohemian in a glamorous costume or your witchy best!

It is always fun to mix up a special celebratory brew for the Samhain. In the same way that our Wicca forefather, Gerald Gardner, referred to his Book of Shadows as a "recipe book," you, too, can create and design recipes for food, drink, incense, and essential oil blends for your festival. I often collect recipes in my Book of Shadows and keep a plentitude of notes and musings in the back of the book. I check for any associations and correspondences (see pages 116–137) and adapt the recipe for the occasion.

## *Samhain Incense Recipe*

Samhain, when the veil between realms is at its thinnest, is a time to honor ancestors, spirits, and loved ones on the other side. Our beloved dead are very responsive to scent and this smoky blend will help you express gratitude and commune with the dear departed.

### GATHER TOGETHER

10 cinnamon sticks

Mortar and pestle

¼ cup of cloves

⅓ cup pumpkin seeds

½ cup finely chopped ginger

⅓ cup myrrh resin

1 tablespoon amber resin

¼ cup frankincense resin

Break the cinnamon sticks into small pieces and place in the mortar with the cloves and pumpkin seeds. Grind down to a powder with the pestle. Now fold in the ginger. Finally, add the myrrh, amber, and frankincense and lightly grind to a powder.

To use the powdered incense straight away, see the instructions for the Self-Assurance Charm for Creativity (page 28). Alternatively, store the powder to be burned in rituals throughout the year. Its strong scent is particularly perfect for use in the All Hallows Ritual (see opposite).

# *All Hallows Ritual*

Bring only your best to this night. After all, All Hallows is New Year's
Eve for witches, and you want to truly connect with those who have
gone on to the other side. This ritual can be performed as a solo spell,
or as a shared experience with your tribe. If you invite others to
participate, make sure you have enough wine, goblets, and bread
to share in the sacrament.

## GATHER TOGETHER

Stone altar

Chalk

Powdered incense (see box, left)

13 candles (in yellow, orange,
and gold colors)

Black cloth

Bread, on a small plate

Salt, in a small dish

Red wine, in a goblet

Matches

If you have invited guests, prepare the altar before they arrive by setting
out a Triple Goddess design (see following page) in chalk on the stone
altar. In the central circle, draw a pentagram.

Set the incense in the center of the pentagram (to use the powdered
incense, see the instructions for the Self-Assurance Charm for Creativity,
see page 28) and place a candle on each of the five points. Arrange the
rest of the candles around the moons on each side. On the black cloth
in front of the altar, place the bread, salt, and wine.

After you have made your preparations for the altar, ready yourself
by bathing and meditating. Dress in a robe or gown befitting this night,
when the veil between the worlds is at its thinnest. As you ready your
body, mind, and spirit, consider what has taken place in the preceding
year. Cleanse your mind and heart of old sorrows and most especially
of anger and petty resentment.

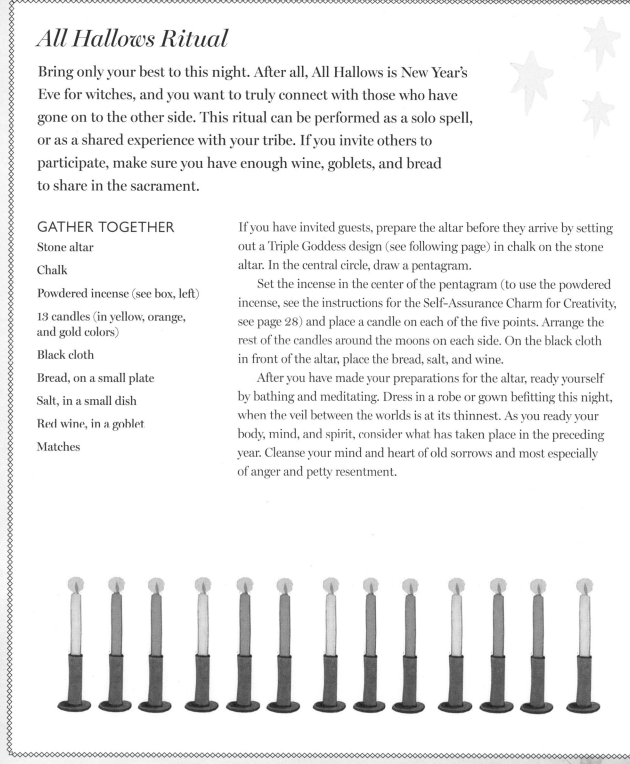

When your guests (if any) arrive, and you are ready to begin, walk alone to the place of the ceremony and kneel before the altar. As you light three of the candles with the matches, say aloud:

*This candle I light for the Maiden's brightest glory.*
Light a candle and bow to the Maiden.

*This candle I light for the power and passion of the Mother, the Queen.*
Light a candle and bow to the Mother.

*This candle I light for the unsurpassable wisdom of the Crone.*
Light the candle and bow to the Crone.

Now, light the incense inside the pentagram. Facing the altar, say aloud:

*These do I light in honor of the Triple Goddess on this sacred night of Samhain.*

*I create this holy temple in honor of the Goddess and the God*

*And all the ancient ones.*

*From time before time,*

*I pay my tribute and my devotion*

*In love and greeting to those behind the veil.*

Now light the rest of the candles and arrange them into a circle around the pentagram to represent the Full Moon.

## THE TRIPLE GODDESS

The Triple Goddess has three aspects: the maiden, a young, sweet girl; the mother, who births us all; and the crone, the wise older woman. The three faces of the Triple Goddess are reflected by the Waxing, Full, and Waning phases of the moon.

THE MAIDEN    THE MOTHER    THE CRONE

Rap three times on the altar with your hands or with your wand. Then say:

*This is a time outside of time*

*In a place outside of any place*

*On a day that is not a day*

*Between the worlds and afar.*

Pause and listen to your heart for thirteen beats. Then, hold your hands in benediction over the bread, salt, and wine. Now say:

*For this bread, salt, and wine,*

*I do ask the blessings*

*Of our Maiden, our Mother, and our Crone*

*And of the God who guards the Gates of the World.*

Sprinkle a little salt over the bread and say:

*I ask that I and all whom I love*
*Have health and abundance and blessings.*

If you have invited guests, this is the time to share the bread and the wine with them. Whether you are enacting this rite as a group or alone, you should now meditate and allow yourself to ease into a trance state. Connect with elders, guides, and ancestors on the other side and communicate with your beloved spirits. Listening closely to the messages they have for you.

When you feel the ritual has ended, quench the incense and candles, and say:

*Though these flames*

*Of the material world*

*Be darkened,*

*They shall ever burn*

*In the world beyond.*

*This rite is ended.*

Preserve the altar as it is through the next day and night, to observe the Day of the Dead, on November 1. Record the messages you heard from the other side in your Book of Shadows. These may be thoughts, impressions, new ideas, or inspiration, doubtless sent through the veil between the realms.

# Yule

Pagans are community-oriented by nature. Long ago, in Northern climes, this seasonal festival was based on how best to get through—and, in some cases, survive—times of cold and scarcity by sharing food, sharing supplies, and sharing the nightly fire. These evening gatherings naturally led to much storytelling—many oral cultural traditions were born of fire.

## Winter Solstice Ritual

Winter solstice rituals in the Northern Hemisphere traditionally celebrate the rebirth of the sun. If the weather is mild, you can perform this rite outside, but if it is very cold, choose a room or space with a fireplace to ensure that this community celebration stays both comfortable and comforting as you gather to share your wishes for the warmer days to come.

### GATHER TOGETHER

Table to serve as an altar

White cloth

Large bundle of evergreen

Powdered incense (see page 68)

White votive candles (one for each attendee)

Mugs (one for each attendee)

Large thermos of celebratory drink (such as Bright Blessings Brew, see page 85)

Firewood

Aromatic kindling (such as cedar, cherry, palo santo, pinion, pine, applewood, pear, oak, or birch)

Matches

Ribbons (for lucky colors, see box page 31)

Cover the table with a white cloth and decorate with evergreen. Place the incense, candles, and mugs on the table along with the thermos. Once everyone is comfortably gathered, welcome folks and take a moment to acknowledge the background of this holiday and rite.

Build and light the fire with the wood, kindling, and matches, and light the candles and incense while the fire begins to build. (To use the powdered incense, see the instructions for Self-Assurance Charm for Creativity, page 28.)

Using a couple of strands of the evergreens from the altar, fashion the branches into a crown, and secure with ribbon. Invite each participant to do the same. When everyone is wearing their crowns, form a semicircle around the fire. Now, say aloud:

*As the sun returns, back to the earth,*

*We gather here for shared joy and mirth,*

*We commemorate life and death and rebirth.*

*Cold winter nights, frozen days so bright,*

*A time of magic, at this longest night,*

*Without the dark, there cannot be light.*

*Thank you for the sun that gives us life,*

*Without beginning and without end,*

*With gratitude on this Solstice night,*

*So mote it be! Blessed be!*

Now, ask those gathered to serve themselves a drink, and to share their hope and wishes for the coming spring. When the sharing winds down, close the ritual with a toast to the Winter Solstice.

*Blessed be to the Mother Goddess and Father God.*

*We live in your light!*

*Everlasting in Eternity.*

*This ritual is now done!*

As you pack up the mugs and other ritual elements, send the participants home with their herbal crowns and a candle each, as a memento of this sacred occasion and collective experience.

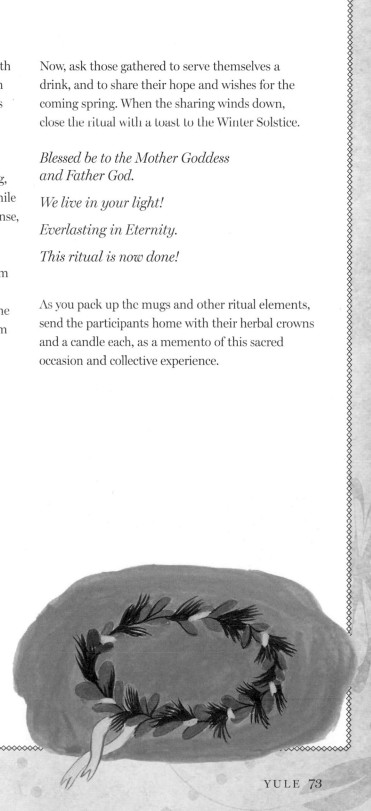

# Imbolc

Imbolc is a celebration of rebirth and renewal, traditionally held on February 1. In the Northern Hemisphere, it is a harbinger of spring, the midpoint between the winter solstice and the spring equinox).

Imbolc is also known as St Brigid's Day. It is said that St Brigid is a Christianization of the Celtic goddess, Brid, who was famous for her poetry, wisdom, and her care for others. In honor of Brid's protective qualities, St Brigid's day is a wonderful opportunity to honor new witches in your circle, and many Wiccans use the Imbolc sabbat to initiate new witches and acknowledge their progress on the path.

## Brigid's Bowl: Creamy Potato Soup

This recipe makes 6–8 cups of soup, but the ingredients can be doubled (or tripled!) as needed. This seasonal soup will warm body, heart, and soul.

During the winter, many of our tribal forebears relied on food they had preserved and stored, like salted, dried fish or meat, cheeses, and fruits such as apples. Root vegetables like beets and potatoes provided sustenance during the bitter, long winters. This potato soup recipe is perfect for an Imbolc celebration or initiation ceremony. It is a wonderful way to pay tribute to the hedge witches, hunters, gatherers, and gardeners who came before us and ensured the survival of their neighbors through hard work, practicality, and strong, generous hearts.

## GATHER TOGETHER

Large saucepan

4 cups (900ml) chicken stock

4 cups (900ml) milk

8 tablespoons butter

Large pot

1 cup (140g) flour

6 bay leaves

½ teaspoon freshly ground black pepper

4 large baking potatoes, peeled and finely diced

1 teaspoon salt

6–8 small ovenproof bowls

Sour cream, to serve

Shredded Cheddar cheese, to serve

Green (spring) onions, to serve

Crispy bacon, to garnish (if desired)

Spoons, for serving

In a large saucepan, gently warm the chicken stock and milk over a medium-high heat.

Melt the butter in a large pot. Add the flour, stirring constantly, to form a roux. Slowly add the stock and milk mixture, stirring vigorously to combine. Add bay leaves, pepper, potatoes, and salt. Simmer over a low heat for 15–20 minutes.

When the potatoes are tender and the soup has thickened, stir, lightly mashing the potatoes in the soup. Pour the soup into the bowls and top with sour cream, Cheddar cheese, and green (spring) onions.

Heat the broiler (grill) to low. Put the bowls on a baking sheet and broil for 1–2 minutes, until golden and bubbling. Garnish with crispy bacon (if using), and serve with the spoons.

Enjoy the merriment, the feasting, and the friendship and make sure to track all in your Book of Shadows.

# Ostara

Ostara celebrates the spring equinox on March 21, as the sun warms the Northern Hemisphere and spring approaches.

Ostara, or Ēostre, the Saxon goddess, is the personification of the rising sun and is associated with the coming spring and radiant dawn. In some languages her namesake is also known as the festival of Easter and legend has it that her totem—the rabbit—brought forth the brightly colored eggs now associated with this festival.

## Spring Equinox Divination

Invite your guests to this simple and humble ritual, which befits the purity of the equinox. This spell invokes the Full Moon's divinatory powers (see page 56) to bring fresh inspiration and intentions for the seasons ahead. The four white candles represent each of the seasons, while the round, white bowl represents the Full Moon.

## GATHER TOGETHER

Small table, for an altar

4 white candles

Matches

White spring flowers (such as crocus, lily, or snowdrop)

Round, white bowl of freshly drawn water

Bay laurel leaves, one for each attendee, in a basket

Invite all the attendees to take a seat in a circle around the altar. Light the candles with the matches. Scatter the white flowers in the bowl of water.

Pass the bowl and the basket of leaves around the circle. Invite each ritualist, one by one, to dip a leaf into the bowl of water, then touch the wet leaf to the third eye (located on the forehead). Each attendee should pass the basket of herbs and the bowl on to the next person until everyone has anointed their third eye.

Now, each ritualist should clap resoundingly and say in turn:

*And now it is done; now it is spring!*

*It is spring in the East,*

*It is spring in the South,*

*It is spring in the West,*

*And it is spring in the North!*

*Blessed be we and thee!*

Invite people to sit comfortably and share their insights and epiphanies, as the spirit moves them. These visions and new ideas will be important to share in your Book of Shadows and review when the season changes.

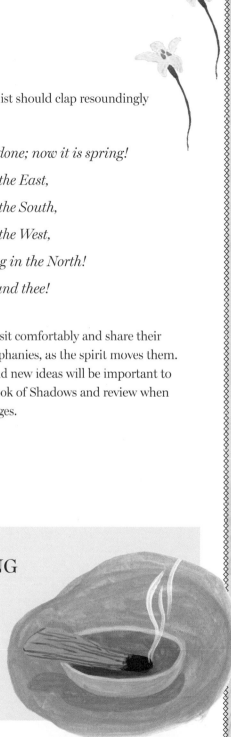

## SWEETEST SPRING SMOKE CLEARING

Power up this equinox enchantment by smudging the room with powerful herbal scents. Braided sheaves of sweetgrass, for example, have been burned in rituals for centuries to call forth ancestors and send away unwanted energy. For more herbal correspondences, see pages 122–123.

# Beltane

Witchy ones celebrate Beltane on the very last eve of April, and it is traditional for the festivities to go on all night. When the sun returns the following day—May Day—revelers erect a beribboned Maypole and dance around in most fanciful garb.

This is a holiday for feasting, laughter, and lots of flirty fun. Dancing is followed by Pagan picnicking and relaxing togetherness. Celebrate this joyous seasonal event with a May Day picnic and bring plenty of mead, beer, wine, cider, and honey mead (which you can make or obtain from a local brewery), or adapt the Bright Blessings Brew (see page 85).

## *May Day Picnic*

Host a joyful spree to look forward to every May. The ribbons in this simple ritual represent the Maypole, a charming May Day tradition that continues after hundreds of years.

Ask your fellow Pagan guests to bring easy-to-eat finger food and a colorful blanket for picnicking. Floral offerings of the spring season should also be in plenitude. Narcissus, daffodils, tulips, and (my favorite) freesias in bright, showy colors, are floral offerings to the gods and goddesses that provide us with such bounty and beauty.

Beltane should be about sheer enjoyment so keeping it simple will reduce the labor and abet the pleasure. At the end of the ritual, ask participants to clean up, compost, and recycle to make sure your event is sacred and sustainable.

## GATHER TOGETHER

Large picnic table, for an outdoor altar

Colorful, floral print tablecloth

Compostable serveware
(like napkins, cups, plates, and sporks)

Multicolored ribbons

Floral incense (such as lavender, rosemary, jasmine, freesia, lilac, gardenia, or rose)

Matches

Fireproof dish

3 large cauldrons half-filled with water to serve as vases for the flowers

Blankets and spreads for seating

Adorn the table with the cloth. Have your guests place their food and drinks on the altar alongside the serveware.

At the altar, offer the guests a ribbon or two to wear as headbands. As they tie the ribbons in their hair, they should speak aloud a wish for this new season of life. Each wish should come directly from the heart—it can be as simple as: "May this spring be bountiful so all may be fed."

Once everyone is adorned with ribbons and has spoken a personal intention, light the incense with the matches and place on the altar in a fireproof dish. As the spring smoke billows and perfumes the air, ask the guests to form a circle and sing the Beltane blessing:

*Hoof and horn, hoof and horn,*

*Tonight our spirits are reborn,*

*Welcome joy into my home.*

*Fill my friends with love and laughter.*

*So mote it be.*

Repeat the blessing twice. While everyone is still holding hands, ask each person around the circle in turn how they can bring more love into the world. Once done, repeat the blessing, and with the last "So mote it be," declare it to be feasting time. Be sure to drink in every drop of joy in this celebration— enough to last for the rest of the year!

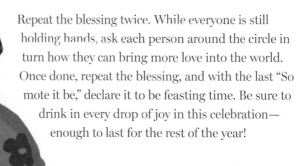

# Litha

In the Northern Hemisphere, the summer solstice takes place on June 21 and is truly a time to remember all the sheer abundance that our earth provides us. I have been heartened to see the increasing popularity of this joyous midsummer thanksgiving in recent years.

Let the season inspire you and gather information about the burgeoning herbs, flowers, and trees all around you. From our flourishing gardens to the bounty of our fields and forests, Litha is a wonderful season to witness the dual energy personified in Wicca tradition as the Lord and Lady of Magic (see box). Record your expressions of appreciation in your Book of Shadows or show your gratitude with a thanksgiving prayer.

## THE LORD AND LADY OF MAGIC

Wiccan tradition frequently addresses twin deities—dual energies that represent the twofold principles of feminine and masculine energy inherent in nature. This sacred connection to Earth and spirit can be traced far back in history to Paleolithic peoples, who worshipped a hunter god and a fertility goddess.

The God is represented by the Sun. He is born on December 21 (the winter solstice) and grows steadily until June 21 (the summer solstice), when his power reaches its fullest. After midsummer (Litha), his power wanes and he expires with the shortening daylight hours. On the longest night of the year, he is reborn again. The energy of the God can be felt in the physical and tangible. He can be seen in the hunt, in the harvest, and in vitality, strength, sexuality, and passion.

The Goddess is creator of all. This Great Mother is the keeper of the cycles of birth, life, death, and rebirth that are reflected in nature and the seasons. In some modern traditions, the God rules the physical world while the Goddess governs intuition, dreams, and the mind.

Wicca is enormously popular today, in part because it gives us freedom to create our own way of worshipping. By understanding the primal, dual aspect of nature, and seeing the world as revealed in these twin mysteries and myths, you can plan rituals that are customized to fit your truest nature.

# Prayer to the Lord and Lady of Magic

Ask your fellow Pagan celebrants to bring an offering to this solstice gratitude ritual, to show thankfulness and appreciation for all received from these beneficent beings—flowers, fruit, a few words of gratitude, or perhaps even a verse of poetry.

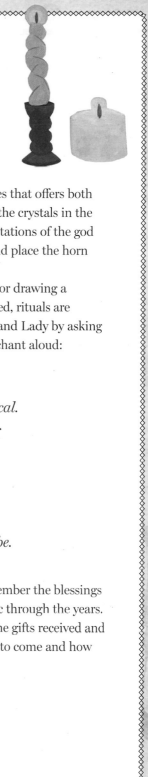

## GATHER TOGETHER

Altar (such as a small stool or table)

Green cloth

Yellow and green crystals (peridot, jade, citrine, quartz, or similar)

Yellow dish

A representation of a god and a goddess (such as a statue, a painting, or an icon of a deity you have made).

2 candles (one green, one yellow)

Matches

Horn (or hollow tree branch), to represent the God

Green bowl, to represent the Goddess

Wand (see pages 108–109)

Set up your altar outside, ideally near a grove of trees that offers both sun and shade, and cover with the green cloth. Put the crystals in the yellow dish and place on the altar with the representations of the god and goddess. Light the candles with the matches and place the horn inside the bowl.

Cast a magic circle with your wand by "casting" or drawing a boundary in the air—inside this circle energy is raised, rituals are performed, and spells are worked. Invoke the Lord and Lady by asking attendees to bring their offering to the altar as you chant aloud:

*O Lord and Lady, wise and true,*

*We will walk with thee in the path to the magical.*

*We thank you for all you have given, life itself.*

*We pledge ourselves to you, here and now,*

*On this sacred summer solstice day.*

*Thanks to you, inspiration we will never lack.*

*With gratitude for all the blessings, so mote it be.*

As the candles burn, everyone gathered should remember the blessings they have received from the Lord and Lady of Magic through the years. Record these blessings in your Book of Shadows—the gifts received and how they have been used for the good, and the gifts to come and how they can be shared in the future.

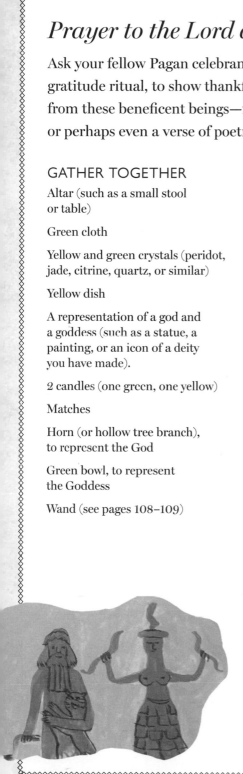

# Lughnasadh

The Celts called this time of the year Lughnasadh, or Lúnasa, for Lugh, a Celtic god of wisdom. Also known as Lammas, this tradition is still celebrated on August 2 far and wide.

Lammas used to be known as "Lammastide," meaning "loaf time," and in the Northern Hemisphere is a celebration of the grain harvest when the grain can be baked into nourishing loaves of bread. The custom is that when the first grain of the season is cut, it must be baked into a loaf and offered to Lugh in a sort of thanksgiving devotion. It is a time of abundance—gather your friends together, be grateful for life's blessings, and record your thoughts and thanksgivings in your Book of Shadows.

## *Lammas Eve Ritual*

Show appreciation for the abundance of nature and the bounty of the harvest with your own unique celebration of the Lammas Day. It is a feast of singing, dancing, storytelling, and celebration, that ends with gratitude and blessings. Don't forget to set a place for the great godly guest, Lugh.

### GATHER TOGETHER

Acorns

Sheaves of grain

Baskets of apples, pears, and oranges

Cauldron

Water (to three-quarter fill the cauldron)

Essential oil (apple, lemon, orange, and pear work well)

Votive candles (one for each attendee)

Matches

Floating candle

Create a sacred space by arranging the acorns, sheaves, and baskets of fruit to the North, South, East, and West of the cauldron. Fill the cauldron with the water and add the essential oil.

Light each of the votive candles with the matches, then hand them to each participant and form a circle around the cauldron. Next, the floating candle should be lit and placed in the cauldron. Speak the following:

*Oh, ancient Lugh of days long past,*

*Be here with us now,*

*In this place between worlds,*

*On this Lammas Day.*

Rap three times on the cauldron. After a few moments, say:

*Harvest is here and the seasons do change.*

*This is the height of the year.*

*The bounty of summer sustains us,*

*In spirit, in soul, and in body.*

Now dance in procession, five times in a spiral around the cauldron. Singing and dancing is a part of this rite, and the procession can end with storytelling and expressions of gratitude for the gifts of the season and the riches of the harvest bounty. Record the songs and stories that you share in your Book of Shadows.

The leader declares when the rite is finished by putting out the candles and proclaiming: "This rite is done."

# Mabon

The sabbat of Mabon represents the end of the fruit, vegetable, and grain harvest in Northern climes. Gathering around a roaring bonfire with ale, wine, mead, and festival foods is the perfect tribal celebration to give thanks for the harvested stores that will provide sustenance and ensure survival through the long, cold winters.

Traditionally celebrated at the Autumn Equinox on September 22, Mabon reminds us of the fact that winter is near and that community is not just about the bonds of family and friendship, but our very survival.

Just as your Book of Shadows is a wonderful way to share experience and knowledge with your coven, Mabon can keep the spirit of food sharing alive in your community. I have an old apple tree that is fruitful, and I have made cider and simple apple sauce with the fruit, packing it in pretty jars with colorful ribbons for my spiritual sisterhood. What can you make and share for the next Mabon observation?

The gift of food keeps cords of connection and community strong. Celebrate Mabon with family, friends, and neighbors, and remember—gatherings are much merrier with a hearty witch's brew (see right)! Pass the blessings on and they will return to you threefold.

## *Bright Blessings Brew*

This cup of comfort is brimming with a marvelous blend of herbs
that not only have immune-boosting antioxidant properties but
also help to brighten your mood and confer a sense of calm.

### GATHER TOGETHER

3 cinnamon sticks

Mixing bowl

1 teaspoon lemongrass

1 teaspoon fennel seeds

1 teaspoon grated lemon zest

2 tablespoons dried rosehips

Wooden spoon

Teapot

Tea kettle

Tea strainer

Mugs

Honey (local, if possible)

Break the cinnamon sticks into pieces and put them into a bowl followed by all the herbs. Stir gently with the wooden spoon and place into the teapot. Fill the kettle with water and, once boiled, pour into the teapot. Let the herbs steep for a half hour. Stir gently with the wooden spoon, strain, and pour into mugs. Add honey, to taste, and serve. To your health!

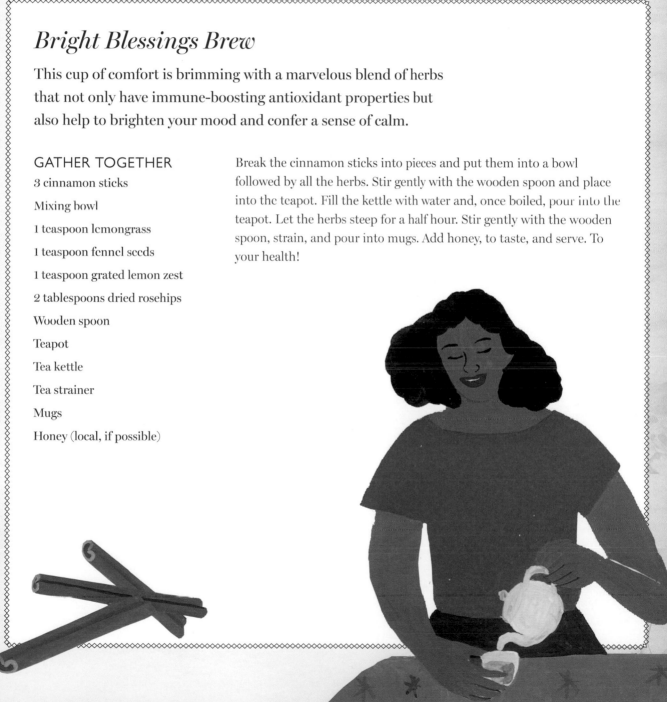

# Chapter 6

# SUN, STARS, AND OTHER ASTROLOGICAL INFLUENCES

The movements of the Sun, Moon, and stars have a mighty influence on the world around us. For centuries, our livelihoods have depended on the success of our crops, plants, and herbs, and it is essential to know when best to sow and harvest. Use the experience and wisdom handed down from our elders—the indispensable information that charts the seasons and the zodiacal forecasting contained therein—to reveal the magical connection between the Earth and sky. Use your Book of Shadows to track how astrological movements can influence your plant magic and spellwork as you walk the Pagan path.

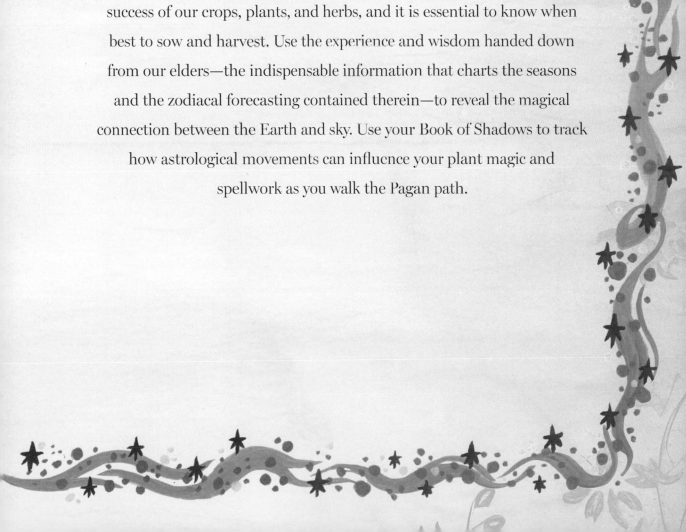

# The Ancient Wisdom of Astrology

The art and science of the stars comes down to us from 6,000 years ago, when the greatest minds of the time—the scholars and scientists, mathematicians and philosophers—co-created what would become the deeply meaningful pursuit of astrology.

The Sumerians, denizens of the "cradle of civilization" in Mesopotamia, were the first to begin mapping the stars and marking their metaphysical meanings. Their neighbors in Ur, the Chaldeans, took this knowledge a step further. They were great record keepers, and they noticed that the recurring patterns tracked in the sky and its constellations helped them to predict what would happen at certain times of the year.

The canny Chaldeans observed certain affinities between the Earth and the sky, between precious gems and "star seasons." These learned people were astronomers, priests, doctors, teachers, and seers, but they were also gemologists, who cut, polished, and studied the gems, rocks, and crystals of their earthly domain. They knew which gems should accompany the dead to the underworld, which rocks portended good fortune when placed over doorways, and which crystals offered benefits to the body. This was just the starting point for a study that would grow and continue for thousands of years, but which provides the basis for today's chemistry, as well as of astrology.

# The Earth and the Sky

Thousands of years before the Big Bang theory, the Chaldeans and Sumerians knew we are all made of the same "stuff." We are all interconnected; the minerals from the meteorites that fall from the heavens are of the same material as our terrestrial rocks; diamonds are the result of millions of years and millions of pounds of pressure on coal, a rather unlovely hunk of earth. The diamond rings on our fingers started out as coal under our feet.

The spectacular process of creation, stemming from the big bang, is still happening. The universe revolves around us in regular cycles and change is happening at every moment. So, like the clever Chaldeans and the scholarly Sumerians, let us see what we can learn from patterns, cycles, and connections between the stars in the sky and the rocks in the earth beneath our feet.

# Astrological Signs and Sacred Stones

As surmised by the Chaldeans and Sumerians (see page 88), we all come from the same material of the universe and there is a great affinity between the gems, rocks, and crystals on the ground and the astrological signs in the stars. Each sign is associated with a planet, and with a corresponding stone or talisman. Using these sacred stones in your spells and charms, and tracking their effects in your Book of Shadows, will greatly improve your magical workings.

## Aries (Mars)

**March 20–April 3:** Sunstone, ruled by Mars, is the talismanic stone for early Aries folks. Red with an incandescent glow, sunstone is a gold-flecked good luck charm.

**April 4–April 18:** The talisman for this half of Aries is bowenite, a mossy green stone of great strength and power. While many of the crystals designated for late Aries are red or pink, the green bowenite signifies the other side of the planet Mars.

## Taurus (Venus)

**April 19–May 2:** The talisman for the first half of Taurus is malachite, which corresponds to Venus. An earthy rock befitting to this earth sign, malachite can be used for scrying.

**May 3–May 19:** Jadeite, the lucky stone for later Taureans, comes in many colors. This stone calms the soul and eases the bones. Jadeite also abets the easy expression of love, enabling you to say what is in your heart honestly and easily.

## Gemini (Mercury)

**May 20–June 4:** Moss agate perfectly represents the dualism of the twin-signed Gemini and is associated with the metal-rich planet Mercury, ruler of the sign of the Twins. Geminis need to keep their feet on the ground, and Moss agate is the perfect grounding talisman for this airy sign.

**June 5–June 20:** Geodes, which usually come in two split halves, help integrate the two parts of the Gemini nature, and make for a complete whole. Geodes are formed from old volcanic bubbles and are usually solid agate with a center of amethyst, opal, or rock crystal. Multifaceted, just like Geminis!

## Cancer (the Moon)

**June 21–July 4:** Pearl is the perfect talisman for those born in early Cancer as these folks are the great historians of the zodiac. With their incredible memories, pearls connect to Cancers through the ocean and the tides, since their ruler, the moon, influences the flow of the waters of the earth.

**July 5–July 21:** Red coral, the talisman for the second half of Cancer, is formed by lime secreted by sea creatures. It is believed to have healing and protective qualities. For Cancers, red coral is a symbol of life, vitality, love, and health.

## Leo (the Sun)

**July 22–August 5:** Early Leos count zircon as their talisman, a stone beloved by early cultures. For Leos, whose fall can be pride, zircon can guard against this and keep astrological Lions on an even keel.

**August 6–August 21:** Heliodor, named for the sun, is the ultimate talismanic stone for late Leos. A member of the beryl family, heliodor is formed under high pressure and temperatures. Heliodor can help Leos call on their greatest qualities and talents to make their dreams come true!

# Virgo (Mercury)

**August 22–September 5:** Early Virgo's talisman is labradorite. Like Geminis, Virgos are also ruled by Mercury, and this quicksilver, peacock-hued crystal is good for mental swiftness. Labradorite can prevent exhaustion for hardworking Virgos.

**September 6–September 22:** Tiger's eye, great for perception and focusing the mind, is the late Virgo talisman. Virgos are the great critics, missing no flaw, and tiger's eye can help them to also have great vision and see wonderful possibilities. Tiger's eye offers protection during travel and strengthens conviction and confidence.

# Libra (Venus)

**September 23–October 6:** Dioptase is the talisman for early Libras. The intensity of this gorgeous green stone makes it a love crystal for Librans, both in the sense of relationships and in the higher love for humankind. Dioptase can awaken the spiritual side of Libras, making this usually attractive sign even more beautiful inside and out.

**October 7–October 22:** Like Taurus, the late Libran's talisman is green jadeite, sometimes called "Imperial Green Jade." In ancient China, it was believed that this type of jade contains all that you need for a long, happy life: courage, modesty, charity, wisdom, and—most importantly to bring Libra scales into balance—justice.

# Scorpio (Pluto)

**October 23–November 6:** Blue fluorite is a stone that heals emotional wounds. Secretive Scorpios carry many hurts beneath their strong exteriors, and over time, fluorite can gently resolve them.

**November 7–November 2:** The birthstone for February-born Aquarians and Pisceans, Amethyst is also the talisman for late Scorpios. The purple color corresponds to (former) planet Pluto and the element of water. Amethyst can open love vibrations for Scorpios, offering a greater chance of happiness for this most misunderstood and enormously powerful sign.

# Sagittarius (Jupiter)

**November 22–December 5:** Formed from fossilized tree sap and resin, organic amber is the talisman for early Sagittarians. Energizing for wildly active Sagittarians, amber helps performers, actors, and musicians.

**December 6–December 20:** Sagittarians are the centaurs of the zodiac, and their turquoise talisman is a strong fit, as it is associated with horses and riders. Turquoise, once revered as the "Eye of Ra," lends great insight and aids travel. It finds purpose, harnesses passion, and maintains the vision to see it through.

# Capricorn (Saturn)

**December 21–January 6:** Lazulite, opaque and displaying the dark, cloudy blue associated with Saturn, is good for mental processes. Dogged and hardworking Capricorns will do well to keep this concentration-enhancing talisman nearby at all times.

**January 7–January 19:** Capricorns sometimes seem slow and plodding to others, but lapis lazuli connotes the wisdom, accomplishment, and value that befits the latter half of this sign. Capricorns are surefooted and careful and will get to the top of the mountain while others fall behind.

# Aquarius (Uranus)

**January 20–February 3:** Moldavite, a mysterious and powerful crystal, is perfect for early Aquarians. These scientist-philosophers are among the greatest thinkers of the zodiac and frequently awe us with their discoveries.

**February 4–February 18:** Diopside brings practicality to intellectual, mathematical, and analytical Aquarians. Late Aquarians also have jade for their talisman, a universal healing and love stone to keep these very intellectual people in touch with their hearts.

# Pisces (Neptune)

**February 19–March 4:** Oceanic aquamarine corresponds to Neptune, the ruling planet of Pisces. Aquamarine is a mutable stone, which changes color when exposed to heat, making it an apt talisman for the dual sign of the Fishes. Aquamarine was once believed to be the dried tears of sea nymphs.

**March 5–March 19:** The talismanic stone for late Pisces is the apple-green chalcedony known as chrysoprase. Associated with sovereignty, this stone has been revered through the ages and utilized by high priests of every era. It is said that chrysoprase brings healing, joy, and laughter, by teaching how to love yourself—as well as your shortcomings.

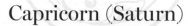

# Planning by the Planets

For millennia, our ancestors have tracked the movements of the stars and planets, using the recurring constellations as a kind of celestial timetable to mark seasonal events, from celebrating sabbats to sowing the harvest (see page 96).

Like our ancestors, you can plan your spells for maximum effect by spellcasting, planting magical herbs, or setting magical intentions during the time of greatest planetary influence for you. The planet that aligns with your astrological sign (see pages 90–93) is likely to have the greatest influence on your magical workings. See the chart (opposite) for the daytime hours that will maximize your powers and ensure success, and don't forget to track your results in your Book of Shadows.

You can also align your magical intentions with the planets. For example, if your ritual is for the purpose of a love spell, use the hour of love goddess, Venus or, for communication charms, use the house of messenger god Mercury.

# MAGICAL HOURS FOR EVERY DAY OF THE WEEK

Follow the planet that corresponds with your astrological sign (see pages 90–93) to find the optimum time of the week to work your magic and ensure success. Leo, for example, corresponds with the sun, and will find their powers at their height early on Sunday morning, as well as various other times throughout the week.

| Hour | Sunday | Monday | Tuesday | Wednesday | Thursday | Friday | Saturday |
|------|--------|--------|---------|-----------|----------|--------|----------|
| 6–7am | Sun | Moon | Mars | Mercury | Jupiter | Venus | Saturn |
| 7–8am | Venus | Saturn | Uranus | Moon | Mars | Mercury | Jupiter |
| 8–9am | Mercury | Jupiter | Neptune | Saturn | Uranus | Moon | Mars |
| 9–10am | Moon | Mars | Pluto | Jupiter | Neptune | Saturn | Uranus |
| 10–11am | Saturn | Uranus | Sun | Mars | Pluto | Jupiter | Neptune |
| 11–12pm | Jupiter | Neptune | Venus | Uranus | Sun | Mars | Pluto |
| 12–1pm | Mars | Pluto | Mercury | Neptune | Venus | Uranus | Sun |
| 1–2pm | Uranus | Sun | Moon | Pluto | Mercury | Neptune | Venus |
| 2–3pm | Neptune | Venus | Saturn | Sun | Moon | Pluto | Mercury |
| 3–4pm | Pluto | Mercury | Jupiter | Venus | Saturn | Sun | Moon |
| 4–5pm | Sun | Moon | Mars | Mercury | Jupiter | Venus | Saturn |
| 5–6pm | Venus | Saturn | Uranus | Moon | Mars | Mercury | Jupiter |

# Sowing by the Signs

Applying practical astrological wisdom to your kitchen garden will ensure you have happy and thriving herbs, flowers, and plants for your spellwork and kitchen witchery.

Growing up on a farm, I have known the powerful effect of astrology since childhood. Many farmers continue to rely on the charts and calendars of the *Old Farmer's Almanac* (1793), which has been published in America since colonial times.

As my birthday mate, Nicolaus Copernicus (born on February 19, 1943), pointed out long ago, the Sun is the center of our planetary system. Earth and the other planets loyally circle "Old Sol," pulled by the gravitational force of the star. Its heat and bulk affect all bodies within a range of nearly a billion miles. Naturally, Fire is the element of our sun and the source of life on our planet. But the Earth, Water, and Air elements have an equally important part to play when it comes to working with the land.

## Earth

Those born under practical Capricorn, Taurus, and Virgo signs are successful types who enjoy helping each other to the top. In the garden, too, it is a productive time to spend with the soil. All three signs are considered very fertile and a great time for planting root crops, such as carrots, turnips, and potatoes. It's also an excellent time for grafting fruit trees, sowing seeds, and planting bulbs. Virgo, a healing sign, is the time to cultivate medicinal plants, and is also perfect for improving the soil and turning compost.

## Water

Folks born under mysterious Cancer, Scorpio, and Pisces are sensitive, passionate, and creative. They are comfortable to swim in the same current. These three signs are considered the most fertile and fruitful signs of the entire zodiac. The best time for planting almost anything falls under the moist conditions of these three signs and it is a great time to work on irrigation. Plants that require strong root development, such as tomatoes, corn, or peppers, are best planted under these signs. Scorpio is an incredible sign for sowing and planting and is exceptionally good for vine growth.

## Fire

Those born under the sign of Leo, Sagittarius, and Aries tend to be bold, courageous, and fun loving. Fire signs are the most barren of the zodiac and, although a few things may surprise you, you'll want to mostly spend these days weeding, controlling pests, pruning, and cultivating the ground. It is said that harvesting under Aries will result in the best keeping, so crops that need to be stored for a long while should be harvested at this time.

## Air

The smart, talkative, and artistic folks born under the signs of Gemini, Libra, and Aquarius speak the same language. Full of energy, the air signs are a good time to harvest and plant for flowers. Like the Fire signs, these times do not particularly favor planting crops, although Libra is still semi-fruitful and a good time to plant vines. It's also a great time to pick a flower crop because they'll last the longest.

# The Witch's Herb Garden

Astrological herbology is a splendid inclusion to your Book of Shadows. Passed down from hedge witches of old to today's modern Pagans, green witchery will greatly inform your understanding of the connection between the sky and the Earth, the stars above and the plants below.

Choose herbs for your altar based on your astrological sign or experiment with the celestial correspondences when making tinctures, incense, oils, potpourri, and other magic potions for your rituals. For example, if the moon is in Aries at the time of your ritual, try using peppermint or fennel, two herbs sacred to the sign of the Ram. Or, if you are creating a special altar while the sun is in the sign of Cancer, use incense, oils, teas, and herbs corresponding to that astrological energy, such as jasmine and lemon. The astrological correspondences create a synthesis of energies that will add impact to your ceremonial work.

# HERBAL CORRESPONDENCES

Below are the herbs that correspond with the astrological signs and their ruling planets. For more herbal magical correspondences, see pages 116–137.

**Aries (Mars):**

Carnation, cedar, clove, cumin, fennel, juniper, peppermint, and pine.

**Taurus (Venus):**

Apple, daisy, lilac, magnolia, oak moss, orchid, plumeria, rose, thyme, tonka bean, vanilla, and violet.

**Gemini (Mercury):**

Almond, bergamot, mint, clover, dill, lavender, lily, and parsley.

**Cancer (the Moon):**

Eucalyptus, gardenia, jasmine, lemon, lotus, rose, myrrh, and sandalwood.

**Leo (the Sun):**

Acacia, cinnamon, heliotrope, nutmeg, orange, and rosemary.

**Virgo (Mercury):**

Almond, bergamot, mint, cypress, mace, moss, and patchouli.

**Libra (Venus):**

Catnip, marjoram, spearmint, sweet pea, thyme, and vanilla.

**Scorpio (Pluto):**

Allspice, basil, cumin, galangal, and ginger.

**Sagittarius (Jupiter):**

Anise, cedarwood, sassafras, star anise, and honeysuckle.

**Capricorn (Saturn):**

Mimosa, vervain, and vetiver.

**Aquarius (Uranus):**

Gum acacia, almond, citron, cypress, lavender, mimosa, peppermint, and pine.

**Pisces (Neptune):**

Anise, catnip, clove, gardenia, lemon, orris, sarsaparilla, and sweet pea.

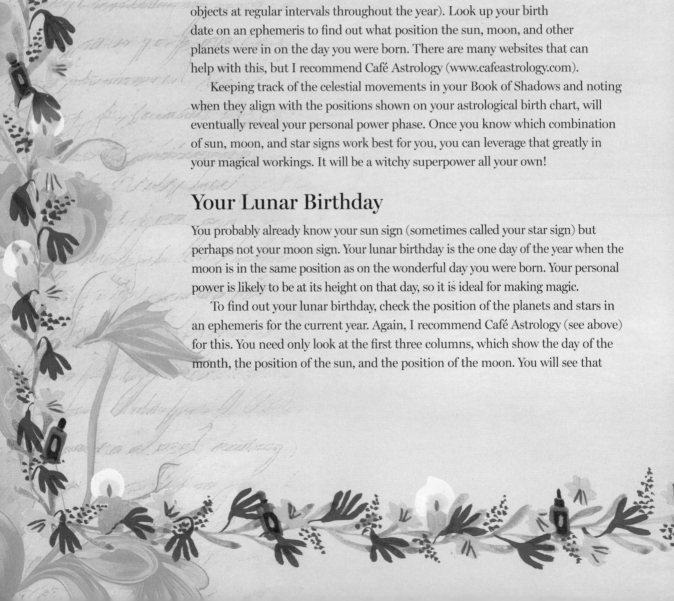

# Personal Power Phase

In much the same way that you manage your garden, plants, and herbs by the signs, you can plan your magical workings by these celestial signs to ensure that they, too, will be fruitful.

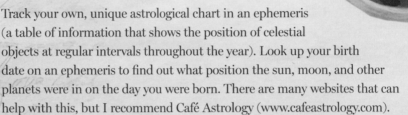

Track your own, unique astrological chart in an ephemeris (a table of information that shows the position of celestial objects at regular intervals throughout the year). Look up your birth date on an ephemeris to find out what position the sun, moon, and other planets were in on the day you were born. There are many websites that can help with this, but I recommend Café Astrology (www.cafeastrology.com).

Keeping track of the celestial movements in your Book of Shadows and noting when they align with the positions shown on your astrological birth chart, will eventually reveal your personal power phase. Once you know which combination of sun, moon, and star signs work best for you, you can leverage that greatly in your magical workings. It will be a witchy superpower all your own!

## Your Lunar Birthday

You probably already know your sun sign (sometimes called your star sign) but perhaps not your moon sign. Your lunar birthday is the one day of the year when the moon is in the same position as on the wonderful day you were born. Your personal power is likely to be at its height on that day, so it is ideal for making magic.

To find out your lunar birthday, check the position of the planets and stars in an ephemeris for the current year. Again, I recommend Café Astrology (see above) for this. You need only look at the first three columns, which show the day of the month, the position of the sun, and the position of the moon. You will see that

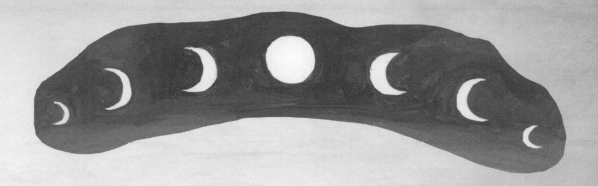

at some point near your birthday, the sun and moon will be in the same signs as when you were born. There may be a few days of crossover, but the one that is your lunar birthday is when the moon is in the same degree or close to it. Each year will vary slightly, and sometimes it will line up with the actual date of your birth.

I highly recommend you note your own astrology chart in your Book of Shadows and use a trusted ephemeris to figure out your lunar birthday every year. This is truly a banner day for you as your magical workings will be super-powered by this astral energy!

## WORKING OUT YOUR LUNAR BIRTHDAY

My psychic, Robin, was born on September 17, with the sun in Virgo at 24° and the moon in Sagittarius at 9°. Let's work out her lunar birthday for 2025. By checking the ephemeris, I can see that the moon is in the same sign as when she was born on September 15, 16, and 17; of those, the moon is closest to 9° on September 16 (when it is at 14°), meaning that in 2025 her lunar birthday is just a day before her solar birthday.

# Chapter 7

# TRACKING YOUR SOLITARY MAGIC

In a way, solo spells are perfectly suited for making the best use of
your Book of Shadows—much more so than group rituals. The magical
workings you track in your Book of Shadows are 100 percent the result of
your own effort and energy, and you can tweak the elements, the timing,
or the lunar and solar influences as you see fit. Like a scientist in a lab,
you can adjust as you go and make modifications—often very small
adjustments—toward achieving your magical intention.

# Developing Your Coven of One

While group ritual is about service and connection, for many folks, solitary ritual comes from the deepest inner rhythms. It comes from your own needs, your own questing, and your own psyche.

The human spirit loves ritual. Observe your own children, or those of your neighborhood, and notice how they create their own spontaneous rituals during play. It seems to be an important part of human development. The inclusion of ritual and celebration in our lives not only enriches us but can also make us healthier, happier people. Group rituals are frequently tied to social events, like holidays, or coming together to help with a problem in the community, such as illness, financial hardship, or difficulties with childcare.

Solitary rituals, on the other hand, can be a major force in your personal development and an incredibly powerful way to enhance your magical evolution. They kindle soul development and spiritual expansion. As Barbara Walker, author of *Women's Rituals* (1990), says: "Meaning develops out of doing." I have known many people who are going through a rough time, for whom ritual was a touchstone and an aid. Ritual can help you not just get through something, but also learn from it, and come out the other side transformed. With personal rituals, you can also address more private matters that you would rather not share with others or broadcast to the community.

Ultimately, there will come a time when you need to design your own ritual as it springs up from the depths of your soul. Here is your opportunity to examine your deepest, inner self. Use the tools described in this chapter to design rituals that are completely unique to you.

## Solo Spells

For the most part, you will know your aim for your spellcasting and your desired purpose and outcome, but there will also be times when you are looking for divine inspiration.

I highly recommend keeping a list of your personal intentions—and their magical correspondences—in your Book of Shadows. The phase of the moon, the day of the week, the color of the candles you use, and much more, all add to the depth and meaning of your ritual. In the following chapter, there is a list of intentions and their cosmic connections to nature, crystals, essential oils, and much more (see pages 116–137). You can draw from this—and you may well have your own intentions to add.

## Focused Intention

Well-defined and focused intentions are the key to success in a life-enhancing ritual. Good results depend upon clarity. If your intention is not crystal clear, you may not achieve the results you are hoping for. Identify your intention, and plan and prepare for your rituals carefully. Gather any essential ingredients and tools together and prepare the space. Do you need to clear the energy of the room and refresh your altar with some housekeeping and smudge?

As you clear the space, you must also clear the clutter in your mind. If you are in a state of inner chaos, or a nagging worry is bothering you, you will not be able to focus, and the outcome will simply not measure up to your expectations. Will it help you relax if you play CDs of instrumental music or sacred chants? Conscious breathing or stretching may also help. You may even want to create an image of your intention with a visualization.

# Your Inner Temple

**Constructing your inner temple is a marvelous visualization that can guide you on a journey deep inside yourself.**

Your inner temple is a wonderful place to get clarity on where you are in life, and where you would like to go. It is the ideal space for crystalizing your magical intentions—what are the deepest, most personal dreams and wishes that you would like to see come true in your life?

Sit or lie down in a position that is comfortable enough to be relaxing, but not so comfortable as to allow you to drift off to sleep. As you breathe slowly and rhythmically, imagine a peaceful, beautiful place that is pleasing to you. It might be a white, marble temple in a garden under a still, blue sky or a mirrored pool by a sacred grove. It can be any size or shape but should have certain aspects (see right) that will help you understand, shape, and manifest your deepest desires.

**The center:** Your inner temple should have a single center, from which you can access all areas of the temple. This center is a representation of your personal power.

**A reflective surface:** This is a place inside your inner temple where you can look at your spiritual self. The reflective surface might be a scrying mirror, a crystal ball, or even a pool of water. You can use it to see the past, present, and future.

**Water:** Your inner temple can have any number of water sources, such as a well or waterfall, a stream, or even an ocean. Water represents our deepest levels of consciousness. Commune with your deepest self here.

**Earth:** Here is where you ground yourself, take stock of your desires and goals, and create manifestation. It might be a garden, a forest, a meadow, or wherever your imagination guides you.

**Doorways or gates:** Ideally, your inner temple will have four doorways or gates, one for each of the four directions (North, South, East, and West) and elements (Earth, Air, Water, and Fire).

# Directing Your Personal Energy

Once you have clarified your magical intentions, ready your heart and mind for making magic.

Candles are a superb way to get in the zone when preparing for a spell or ritual, and candle magic is my go-to for centering. A meditation, like the ones shown on pages 110–113, is a profound way to focus on and direct your magical intentions.

Wands also direct energy. Druids and Pagans have used wands for this purpose (and to draw a circle of magic, see page 81) for hundreds of years. Today, millions of people are inspired by the wands of fictional magic practitioners, such as Gandalf and Harry Potter. There are many who have found their way to the path of magic through the pages of books. Draw on your own creativity and inspiration to make a unique, personal wand forged by your own hand.

## DIY Wand

Make your own magic wand to bring your unique personality, energy, and intention to your craft.

### GATHER TOGETHER

Fallen branch or twig

Drop cloth or paper towel

Fine sandpaper

Clear varnish or leftover paint

Paintbrush

Hot glue gun

Large, pointed crystal

Glue sticks

Small crystals and beads

If you have a favorite sacred grove, local park, or woodland, take a stroll amongst the trees. Look for a fallen branch or sturdy twig on the ground—one with a larger end where the branch was once attached to the tree is ideal. If it feels good in your hand and is of a length that pleases you, take it home with you.

Lay the drop cloth or paper towel over a crafting table. If your branch has any sharp edges or areas that might scrape your hand or skin, sand them off with the fine sandpaper. If your branch comes from a pretty wood that you find appealing, leave it as is, or paint with a clear varnish. This more natural feel will connect your magic to the energy of the tree and grove where you found it. Alternatively, paint the branch with a color that expresses the look and energy you want for your wand. Let the paint or varnish dry completely.

Using a hot glue gun, affix the large, pointed crystal at the thin, pointed end of the branch. Let the glue dry completely. Once dry, dab glue around the

thicker end with the glue sticks. Stick on color beads and tiny crystals to form a handle. Your new wand is now a colorful object of beauty!

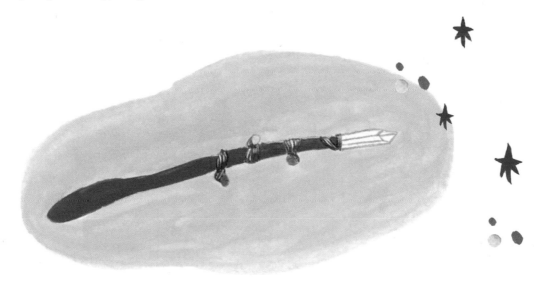

# Lighting Your Path to Magic

Take a simple meditation a step further with this spell for bringing new insight into your life. Use your favorite meditation incense—for me, the gently soothing scent of sandalwood immediately sanctifies any space and creates a sacred aura.

## GATHER TOGETHER

Small, white votive candle

Incense

Matches

Fireproof dish

Athame (or ritual knife)

Place the candle on your altar or "centering station." Light the incense with the matches and place in a fireproof dish next to the candle. Scratch your name into the candle with the tip of your knife and then scratch your hope or intention onto the candle. Light the candle with the matches and recite:

*As I step into the path of magic,*

*I light this flame to guide my way.*

*This candle burns for me.*

*Here burns my hope for [your intention].*

*Here burns the flame of insight,*

*May I see clearly in this new light.*

*So mote it be.*

Sit with your eyes closed for a few minutes. Set your intention by picturing yourself enacting your hopes and desires. Imagine yourself in the company of people who inspire and teach you, who bring insight and new light into your life. Let the candle burn down completely.

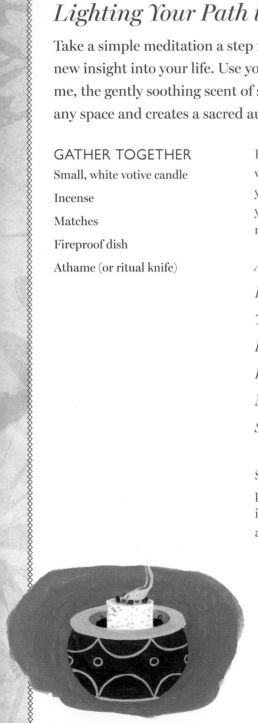

# Centering Meditation

One way to prepare for personal ritual is to center yourself.
I call this "doing a readjustment"—something I believe is
especially important in our overscheduled and busy world.

Take a comfortable sitting position and find your pulse. Feel the steady
rhythm of your own heart. Now begin slowly breathing in rhythm with
your heartbeat. Inhale for four heartbeats, hold for four heartbeats, and
then exhale for five heartbeats. Repeat this pattern for six cycles.

It may seem hard to match your breath with the heartbeat at first, but
with a little bit of practice, they will synchronize. Your entire body will relax,
and once you are truly centered, your body and mind will align. Doing a
readjustment will help you to get your priorities back on track so you can
do the true inner work of self-development that is at the core of ritual.

# Invoking the Deities

Invoking deities in your solo spellcraft is a marvelous way to amplify the power and effectiveness of your workings.

In your Book of Shadows, keep a close record of which gods and goddesses abet your magic the most. Recently, I discovered that Quan Yin is a powerful ally for me. I was quite surprised and delighted about this discovery. I had an extremely difficult personal crisis and needed quick and mighty help. I studied how to invoke her and asked for a miracle, via a Buddhist invocation derived from ancient China. Within an hour of calling to Quan Yin, the resolution to my calamity came forward.

By tracking your work with the deities in your Book of Shadows, you may be surprised at which of these immortals abet your magic. The more you know, the more you can access and work with these powerful divinities, discovering personal affinities with various gods and goddesses that will reveal themselves along the way. Find your helpers! They are there and awaiting your invitation.

## *Candle Ceremony*

Before you embark upon this rite, take time to carefully select the deity with whom you feel a connection or who you believe will be benevolent toward your intention (see page 137). Those from other realms or heavenly spheres are very responsive to scent. Ancient and natural fragrances such as frankincense, myrrh, cinnamon, copal, pine, spruce, juniper, or cedar—are optimal for this invocation.

### GATHER TOGETHER

1 candle, in your deity's favorite color

Athame (or ritual knife)

Cinnamon essential oil

Small table or three-legged stool, for an altar

Incense

Fireproof dish

A representation of your chosen deity (such as a statue, a painting, or an icon of a deity you have made)

Paper and pen

Matches

Carve symbols and power words related to your deity into your candle with the tip of the knife. Anoint the candle with the essential oil. Dressing the candle from top to bottom adds the influence of attraction to your spell. Conversely, dressing the oil in the opposite direction, bottom to top, adds banishing power to your spell.

Position the small table or stool in the place where you wish to carry out the invocation, and arrange the candle, incense in a fireproof dish, and the representation of the deity on top. With the pen, write your intention on the paper, and then speak aloud:

*Power of the Heavens,*

*Power of the Earth.*

*I come to you on this day,*

*I come to you with a heart full of love.*

*Thus I consecrate this candle in the name of* [deity's name],

*So this flame will burn brightly and light my way.*

Place the anointed candle in the candleholder, light it with the matches, and say:

*Blessed candle, light of the Goddess,*

*I burn this light of* [deity's name].

*Hear my prayer, O* [deity's name], *hear my need.*

*Do so with all your grace,*

*Do so with all your wisdom.*

*Do so with all your power,*

*And magical speed.*

*And so it is.*

Now read your intention as you wrote it on the paper. Roll the paper into a scroll and, using a few drops of warm wax from your candle, seal your sacred statement. Place the paper on your altar and allow the candle to burn down completely.

Transfer all the items from your invocation altar to your main altar in the room where you do most of your magical workings. The energy of the deity will also grace that space while the invocation works its magic.

When the spell comes to culmination—once your intention is realized—locate the scroll and burn the written intention in a fireproof dish or in your fireplace, to show gratitude to the god or goddess who helped you.

# Moon Magic

When I first started on the path, all my rites were solitary because there was no real community of Pagans where I grew up in Appalachia. It was a great way to start out—by tracking my spellwork in a Book of Shadows, I slowly but surely deepened my magical practice over the years. Some of my solo spellcasting mainstays were the monthly Full Moons. To me, they are akin to high holidays and offer many opportunities for rituals and observance you can do on your own.

**January** (**Wolf Moon or Cold Moon**): A good time for communing with your higher spiritual power and reflecting inward. Look back through the pages of last year's Book of Shadows to decide what magical workings you want to carry forward in the seasons ahead.

**February** (**Snow Moon, Hunger Moon, Ice Moon, or Quickening Moon**): This is the season of Imbolc (see page 74), a time of new beginnings, and an opportunity to think about what you would like to accomplish during the coming season.

**March** (**Storm Moon or Worm Moon**): Around the season of Ostara (see page 76), the March Full Moon is a good time to plant the seeds that will bring the things you want into your life. Reflect on the Vernal Equinox of last year by re-reading your Book of Shadows notes and plant seeds for what you want in your life.

**April** (**Wind Moon or Pink Moon**): The first Full Moon of April is a season of love and the season of Beltane (see page 78). April is a good time to focus on romantic relationships and flourishing friendships, and to take continued actions toward your goals.

**May** (**Flower Moon**): Look at tending to your own life, including relationships, career, and self-care. Take action to make sure the seeds you planted continue to grow and thrive.

**June** (**Strawberry Moon or Honey Moon**): One of the biggest and brightest moons of the whole year, Mother Nature offers all her gifts during this month. Take advantage of the bounty and give thanks for the abundance during this Litha season (see page 80).

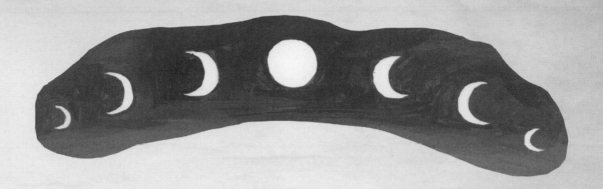

**July (Meadow Moon, Blessing Moon, or Buck Moon):** The warmest month of the year in the Northern Hemisphere, our sun, Old Sol, is shining down upon us all. It is a good time to relax, meditate, and reflect on how you can bring more positive energy into your life.

**August (Corn Moon or Sturgeon Moon):** Appreciate the abundance and joy in the air and celebrate the work and toil of the past months, as thoughts turn to planning for challenging times ahead. During this Lughnasadh season (see page 82), think of what you want to reap in the future and note plans in your Book of Shadows.

**September (Harvest Moon or Wine Moon):** Celebrate the balance of light and dark at Mabon (see page 84). As the Wheel of the Year comes to an end it also a good time to give thanks for all the blessings in your life.

**October (Hunter's Moon or Blood Moon):** A good time to honor loved ones who have passed on. An opportunity to do spiritual and physical cleansing and get rid of what doesn't serve you in the coming year, be that bad habits or clutter in your home. This most sacred Samhain season (see page 84) can be commemorated in our Book of Shadows for future contemplation.

**November (Beaver Moon or Freezing Moon):** Community is more important than ever during the first Full Moon of the Wheel of the Year, November is a good time to cultivate healthy habits and continue to let go of negative energy. Clearing and cleansing spells are very important now.

**December (Cold Moon or Frost Moon):** The December Full Moon is an opportunity to share stories and knowledge. Celebrate Yule (see page 72) and spend time with family and friends.

Chapter 8

# ENHANCING YOUR ENCHANTMENTS WITH MAGICAL CORRESPONDENCES

In many magical traditions, practitioners use what are
known as "correspondences"—symbolic links between an item
(such as a stone or crystal, a flower or herb, or even certain animals)
and your magical intention. Incorporate as many cosmic connections
as you can into your workings to power up your magic and enhance
the results of your spellwork.

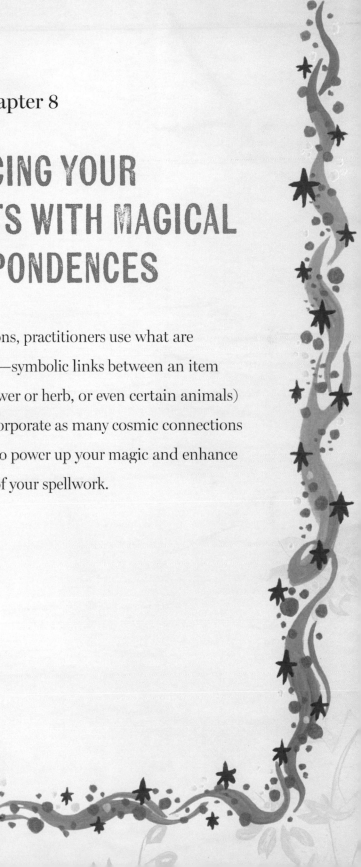

# Cosmic Connections

Those who came before us on the Pagan path have been gathering magical correspondences for millennia. This immensely useful body of knowledge has been passed down to us over the centuries and we owe these scholars and pioneers much gratitude.

Today, magical correspondences can be presented in a handy table format, so the information is accessible and easy to read. Of course, your Book of Shadows is the ideal place to keep these lists and tables, so you can simply flip to that information when you need it. For example, you might find yourself in urgent need of abundance. To prepare for this money magic, you can incorporate herbs, essential oils, incense, crystals, lunar phases, and other correspondences that relate to prosperity into your spells, to create a successful abundance ritual.

You may well have a good working knowledge of these elements and influences already, but it is a really good idea to try new correspondences in your rituals regularly, and carefully record the results in your Book of Shadows. This will determine which ones work especially well for you. Using your Book of Shadows consistently, over time, will result in your own custom tables of correspondence. This is one of the most exciting aspects of keeping a Book of Shadows. Keep an open, curious mind and you are bound to discover the correspondences that are most powerful for you, and which enhance your unique craft.

# Trees

Trees are one of Mother Nature's greatest gifts and are the very lungs of our planet Earth. They provide us with so much—not only food, shelter, shade, sap for essential oils and incense, and tools such as wands, but also the air we breathe. Certain trees can even function as familiars in our life, as does my beloved old apple tree.

Rediscover the beauty and sacredness of nature and get reacquainted with the trees in your own back yard, neighborhood, and nearby parks, forests, groves, and orchards. Paying attention to your local trees and tracking their role in your Book of Shadows will reveal your tree allies to you, deepen your tree wisdom, and help take your magic to the next level.

**Acacia:** Clairvoyance, divination, visions, wealth, and protection.

**Alder:** Banishing, transformation, truth, and intuition.

**Apple:** Dreams, fertility, love, luck, and harmony.

**Birch:** Protection (especially defensive magic), concentration, and creativity. Alleviates anxiety.

**Cedar:** Clairvoyance (especially the afterlife) and psychic ability. Alleviates hexes.

**Cypress:** Protection (especially binding and defensive magic), comfort, mental ability, and wisdom.

**Elder:** Grounding, healing, love, and success.

**Elm:** Intuition, love, pregnancy and childbirth, and stability.

**Juniper:** Fertility, happiness, protection, optimism, and strength.

**Oak:** Confidence, justice, luck, money, success, independence, and wealth.

**Pine:** Beginnings, hope, prosperity, and freedom.

**Rowan:** Devotion, guidance, and psychic ability (especially visions).

**Willow:** Protection, knowledge, and fertility.

**Witch Hazel:** Healing, inspiration, willpower, fidelity, and wisdom.

# The Magical Language of Flowers

Witches and wise women have used flowers and plants in magical rituals for many centuries. Simple charms using a single flower can be some of the quickest of spells. Magical floral associations are myriad—I have an exhaustive list of hundreds of flora in my Book of Shadows, which many people have told me they find overwhelming, so below is a more concise and easy-to-use reference.

**Acacia:** Love (especially chaste and secret), and elegance.

**Almond (flowering):** Hope.

**Allspice:** Compassion.

**Aloe:** Grief and affection.

**Balm of Gilead:** Alleviates illness.

**Beech:** Prosperity.

**Black poplar:** Courage.

**Bluebell:** Kindness, luck, love, manifestation, and overcoming obstacles.

**Cabbage:** Prosperity (especially money).

**Campanula:** Gratitude.

**Canary grass:** Perseverance.

**Carnation:** Love, beauty, communication, fertility, harmony, and emotional balance.

**Cedar:** Strength.

**Celandine:** Joy (especially those to come).

**Centaury:** Happiness.

**Daffodil:** Attraction (especially of fairies and spirits), love (especially unrequited), security, and calm.

**Daisy:** Innocence and mental ability (especially memory and the unconscious mind).

**Dandelion:** Divination.

**Dittany of Crete:** Birth.

**Dock:** Patience.

**Elder:** Devotion and zealousness.

**Elm:** Dignity.

**Forget-me-not:** Love (especially true love).

**Garden chervil:** Sincerity.

**Garden sage:** Esteem.

**Geranium:** Friendship.

**Gillyflower:** Beauty (especially enduring).

**Gladiolus:** Strength.

**Glory flower:** Beauty.

**Gloxinia:** Pride.

**Gorse:** Affection (especially enduring).

**Hawksbeard:** Protection.

**Hawkweed:** Mental ability (especially quick-sightedness).

**Hawthorne:** Hope.

**Hibiscus:** Persuasion.

**Holly:** Foresight.

**Honeysuckle:** Affection, happiness, love, peace, and wellbeing.

**Hyacinth:** Constancy.

**Iceland moss:** Health.

**Jasmine:** Sensuality, grace, and elegance.

**Justicia:** Beauty (especially female).

**Larkspur:** Levity.

**Laurel:** Perfidy and perseverance.

**Lemon blossom:** Fidelity (especially in love).

**Lilac:** Love (especially love's first bloom) and innocence (especially youthful).

**Lily of the valley:** Happiness (especially returning happiness).

**Locust tree:** Elegance.

**Lupin:** Voraciousness.

**Magnolia:** Love (especially of nature).

**Magnolia (laurel-leaved):** Dignity.

**Marigold:** Prediction.

**Marvel of Peru:** Alleviates timidity.

**Meadow lychnis:** Mental ability (especially wit).

**Mercury:** Goodness.

**Nightshade:** Truth.

**Olive:** Peace.

**Orange flowers:** Chastity.

**Orange tree:** Generosity.

**Ranunculus:** Prosperity (especially in charm and relationships).

**Rose:** Fertility, family, love, luck, happiness, and beginnings.

**Scilla (blue):** Forgiveness.

**Snapdragon:** Clairvoyance, emotional balance, money, protection, and assertiveness.

**Snowdrop:** Hope.

**Sorrel:** Affection and joy.

**Stonecrop:** Tranquility.

**Sunflower:** Clarity, dreams, peace, money, and luck.

**Sweet pea:** Freedom and departure (especially letting go), prediction (especially of a meeting), and pleasure.

**Tremella:** Resistance.

**Truffle:** Prediction (especially of a surprise).

**Tulip:** Beauty (especially of the eyes) and love (especially hopeless or a declaration).

**Tussilago:** Justice.

**Valerian:** Flexibility (especially in disposition).

**Verbena (scarlet):** Sensibility.

**Verbena (white):** Purity and innocence.

**Vernal grass:** Happiness.

**Veronica:** Fidelity.

**Virgin's bower:** Love (especially filial).

**Volkmannia:** Happiness.

**White oak:** Independence.

**Willow:** Courage.

**Woodbine:** Love (especially fraternal).

**Xeranthemum:** Alleviates adversity.

**Zephyr flower:** Prediction.

# Healing Herbs

Plants, spices, and herbs hold some of the most valuable and vital healing energy of all witchcraft. Thanks to our Mother Earth's generosity and benevolence, we enjoy a bounty of plants that confer so many benefits from medicine and food to protection and success, and much more. Hedge witches of old developed this knowledge and passed their wisdom to us through the centuries both as lore and through their Book of Shadows. Keep a close note in your Book of Shadows of which herbs work well for you in your rituals and recipes and you, too, can pass your findings to the next generation. I recommend reviewing the herbs you use as each season changes, so you can glean new learning from your magic all through the year.

**Allspice:** Business, luck, success, kindness, and money.

**Angelica:** Divination, purification, and success. Alleviates negativity.

**Anise:** Balance, energy, harmony, purification, and wellbeing.

**Basil:** Psychic ability (especially messages and omens), love (especially reconciliation), money.

**Betony:** Mental ability (especially problem solving), security, and protection. Alleviates anxiety.

**Borage:** Beginnings, business success, courage, and awareness.

**Catnip:** Love, luck, psychic ability, communication with spirits, and wakefulness.

**Chamomile:** Calm, money, and luck. Alleviates anger and anxiety.

**Cinnamon:** Wealth and money, security, luck, desire, attraction, peace.

**Clove:** Divination (especially visions), prosperity, psychic ability, success, and truth.

**Dandelion:** Clairvoyance and divination, clarity, and communication (especially with spirits).

**Dill:** Love, lust, sex, money. Alleviates black magic (especially hexes).

**Fennel:** Alleviates negative energy (especially in the home).

**Garlic:** Justice, protection (especially banishing magic or against hexes), freedom (especially letting go), and security.

**Ginger:** Money, pregnancy and childbirth, unity, and success.

**Ivy:** Attraction, marriage, love, stability, transformation, and fidelity.

**Lavender:** Love, manifestation, luck, and rebirth. Alleviates anger and anxiety.

**Lemon balm:** Business success, calm, clarity, fertility, and relationships.

**Mugwort:** Psychic ability, communication (especially with spirits or the astral realm), awareness.

**Nettle:** Healing, justice, luck, protection, courage, and confidence.

**Nutmeg:** Luck, love, money, power, attraction, psychic ability, and divination.

**Orris root:** Protection, relationships, love, and sexual attraction.

**Pepper:** Motivation, lust, justice, security (especially binding magic), and strength.

**Peppermint:** Divination (especially dreams and visions), luck, money, and healing.

**Rosemary:** Psychic ability and protection, inner power, and luck.

**Sage:** Clairvoyance (especially visions) and cleansing. Alleviates negativity.

**St John's wort:** Strength, power, money, and prosperity.

**Star anise:** Divination and psychic ability, and purification.

**Strawberry:** Beauty, desire, luck, love, relationships, and divination.

**Thyme:** Healing, happiness, rebirth, protection, and calm.

**Wormwood:** Clairvoyance, dreams, and psychic ability.

**Yarrow:** Defense (especially banishing magic), love (especially heartbreak and marriage), healing, freedom (especially letting go), and strength.

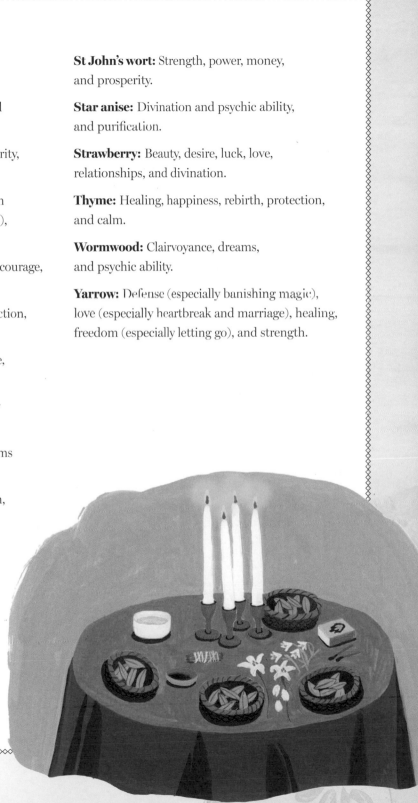

# Enchanted Essences

The global embrace of essential oils—and their healing and calming properties—is endlessly pleasing to me. One of the biggest trends the world over, people simply love essential oils for the uplifting scent and serenity they bring to their homes. These plant-powered essences are immensely useful in so many ways. Knowing which essential oils to use in your spells is vital to your craft. This list matches the essence to the intention of your spell but you can also match the essence to qualities you want to bring to your personal space.

**Acacia:** Meditation and psychic ability.

**Allspice:** Determination, energy, and vitality.

**Amber:** Love (especially as an aphrodisiac).

**Anise:** Divination, clairvoyance, invocation, and protection. Alleviates negativity.

**Apple blossom:** Happiness, relaxation, and success.

**Bay:** Healing and protection.

**Bayberry:** Money and luck (especially in the home).

**Basil:** Love, happiness, harmony, money, peace, protection, prosperity, sympathy, and mental ability (especially quick-thinking). Alleviates negativity (especially spirits).

**Benzoin:** Astral projection.

**Bergamot:** Ability (especially magical), energy, protection, prosperity (when oil is worn in palm of each hand), and money.

**Birch:** Invocation and healing.

**Black pepper:** Courage and protection.

**Camphor:** Cleansing, freedom (especially letting go), meditation, divination, psychic ability, and purification.

**Carnation:** Ability (especially magical), health, energy (especially restorative), love, and power.

**Cedar:** Confidence, invocation, protection (especially from misery and misfortune), prosperity, self-control, and healing.

**Cinnamon:** Concentration, clairvoyance, focus, money, protection, prosperity, psychic ability, sexuality, strength, spirituality, astral projection, and healing.

**Cinquefoil:** Health, love, power, protection, and strength.

**Citronella:** Attraction (especially customers and friends), friendship, purification, and mental ability (especially quick-thinking). Alleviates negativity.

**Clary sage:** Dreams (control and recall). Alleviates depression.

**Clove:** Love (especially as an aphrodisiac), courage, healing, memory, protection, prosperity, sexuality, and divination. Alleviates negativity (especially spirits).

**Cumin seed:** Harmony and peace.

**Cyclamen:** Love (especially marriage) and childbirth.

**Cypress:** Comfort, endings, protection, and transition.

**Dragon's blood:** Ability (especially magical), love, protection, and purification.

**Eucalyptus:** Healing, purification, and protection.

**Frankincense:** Addiction (healing), courage, meditation, protection, purification, and spirituality. Alleviates stress, bad habits, and negativity (especially spirits).

**Gardenia:** Love and protection.

**Geranium:** Love and courage.

**Ginger:** Love (especially as an aphrodisiac), confidence, courage, money, prosperity, passion, lust, and success.

**Heliotrope:** Clairvoyance, meditation, protection, and spirituality.

**Honeysuckle:** Intuition, memory, prosperity, understanding, and mental ability (especially quick-thinking).

**Hyssop:** Purification and money.

**Jasmine:** Love (especially as an aphrodisiac), cleansing, creativity, childbirth, originality, meditation, peace, prosperity, protection, relaxation (especially sleep), spirituality, and astral projection.

**Juniper:** Healing, protection, and purification. Alleviates negativity (especially spirits).

**Lavender:** Awareness, calm, longevity, love (especially as an aphrodisiac), joy, peace, protection, purification, relaxation (especially sleep), health and healing. Alleviates stress, headaches, and depression.

**Lemon:** Ability (especially magical), energy, healing, protection (especially from spirits), and love.

**Lemongrass:** Psychic ability, purification, and sexuality.

**Lilac:** Clairvoyance, decisiveness, harmony, memory, peace, and spirituality.

**Lime:** Energy, purification, healing, protection, and love.

**Lotus:** Happiness, healing, meditation, and prosperity.

**Magnolia:** Harmony, peace, psychic ability, and meditation.

**Mimosa:** Healing and dreams (especially prophetic).

**Mint:** Prosperity.

**Musk:** Confidence, courage, passion, purification, self-assurance, and strength.

**Myrrh:** Healing, meditation, peace, purification, protection (especially from sorrow, evil eye, and hexes), spirituality, and understanding. Alleviates fear and negativity (especially spirits).

**Narcissus:** Harmony, peace, and relaxation.

**Neroli:** Happiness, love (especially as an aphrodisiac), purification, and lust.

**Niaouli:** Healing and protection. Alleviates negativity and curses.

**Nutmeg:** Ability (especially magical), energy, luck, meditation, money, protection, prosperity, psychic ability, relaxation (especially sleep).

**Orange blossom:** Ability (especially magical), love (especially marriage), harmony, purification, and transformation. Alleviates depression.

**Orris root:** Love (especially as an aphrodisiac).

**Patchouli:** Love (especially as an aphrodisiac), energy (restorative), lust, protection, prosperity, money, and sexuality.

**Peony:** Success (especially in business) and prosperity.

**Peppermint:** Ability (especially magical), invocation, prosperity, protection, purification, love, relaxation, sexuality, and transformation. Alleviates negativity (especially spirits).

**Pine:** Ability (especially magical), cleansing, energy, healing, money, protection, prosperity, and purification. Alleviates negativity (especially spirits).

**Pink grapefruit:** Healing, protection, and strength.

**Rose:** Beauty, harmony, love (especially as an aphrodisiac), luck, peace, protection, tranquility, and healing.

**Rose geranium:** Ability (especially magical), courage, happiness, health and healing, and protection.

**Rosemary:** Happiness, healing, invocation, longevity, love, common sense, prudence, protection, memory, self-assurance, sexuality, and vitality. Alleviates negativity (especially spirits).

**Rue:** Protection. Alleviates negativity and curses.

**Sage:** Memory and money.

**Saffron:** Clairvoyance and calm.

**Sandalwood:** Healing, cleansing, protection, and astral projection. Alleviates negativity (especially spirits).

**Sweetgrass:** Transformation.

**Sweet pea:** Attraction (especially customers and friends).

**Tea tree:** Alleviates depression.

**Tuberose:** Peace, love (especially as an aphrodisiac), and psychic ability.

**Vanilla:** Ability (especially magical), energy (especially restorative), happiness, luck, love (especially as an aphrodisiac), lust, and vitality.

**Vervain:** Creativity, prosperity, and protection.

**Vetiver:** Money, luck, love, and protection. Alleviates negativity (especially spirits).

**Violet:** Healing and love.

**Ylang ylang:** Love (especially marriage or as an aphrodisiac), lust, peace, calm, and success (especially in employment). Alleviates negativity.

**Wisteria:** Higher knowledge and illumination.

# Color Correspondences

Every color has a special vibration, which is the source of its power and influence. Use color thoughtfully when choosing candles, flowers, dishes, altar cloths, crystals, and other ritual elements—when certain colors are used in combination with magical intentions, as shown in the list below, great power can be generated in your spells.

You may also find that certain colors work particularly well for you. By tracking the results of your spells in your Book of Shadows, you may discover which colors always seem to guarantee success—these are your power colors and will enhance all your magical workings.

**Red:** Energy and lust.

**Pink:** Love and romance.

**Green:** Prosperity, friendship, and healing.

**Gray:** Protection.

**White:** Purity and new beginnings.

**Blue:** Loyalty, creativity, and vision.

**Orange:** Higher knowledge and enlightenment.

**Purple:** Spirituality.

**Yellow:** Power and fame.

# Gems, Sacred Stones, and Crystals

We witches make frequent use of crystals and gemstones in charms, rituals, and spellwork—every stone has many correspondences and enhancing abilities. While one may offer protection and healing (useful against illness), another may offer protection and courage (ideal for facing your fears), so choose your stone wisely and ensure it is a good fit for the intentions of your spell. Write down which correspondences work best for you in your Book of Shadows, so you can keep track of your results and learn as you go.

**Agate:** Courage, strength, love, and protection.

**Alexandrite:** Luck, love, spiritual transformation, and joy.

**Amazonite:** Success, joy, and self-expression.

**Amber:** Transformation (especially negative energy into positive energy) and protection.

**Amethyst:** Courage, psychic energy, dream control and recall, addiction (healing), intuition, peace, happiness, and love.

**Apache tear:** Protection and luck.

**Aquamarine:** Courage, purification, peace, psychic energy, and self-expression.

**Azurite:** Psychic energy, divination, healing, concentration, and transformation.

**Beryl:** Energy, love, healing, psychic energy, and protection (especially from weather and water).

**Bloodstone:** Courage, strength, victory, wealth, self-confidence, and success (especially in business and legal affairs).

**Calcite:** Centering, grounding, purification, money, and peace. Alleviates fear.

**Carnelian:** Courage, sexual energy, communication (especially verbal), and peace. Alleviates jealousy, apathy, fear, and rage.

**Celestite:** Communication (especially verbal), healing, compassion, and growth. Alleviates stress.

**Chrysocolla:** Wisdom, peace, love, communication, and vitality.

**Chrysoprase:** Prosperity, luck, happiness, friendship, protection, and healing.

**Citrine:** Balance, psychic energy, protection, creativity, and sexual energy. Alleviates nightmares.

**Clear quartz:** Energy and protection.

**Coral:** Protection (especially from conflict).

**Diamond**: Courage, strength, healing, and protection.

**Emerald:** Prosperity, dream control and recall, meditation, love, peace, and balance.

**Fluorite:** Balancing and stabilizing (especially relationships).

**Garnet:** Strength, healing, protection, purification, and compassion.

**Geode:** Fertility, childbirth, meditation, dream control and recall, and astral travel.

**Hematite:** Grounding, calming, healing, divination, intuition, and relaxation (especially sleep).

**Herkimer diamond:** Psychic ability and clairvoyance.

**Infinite:** Communication (especially with angels).

**Iolite:** Accuracy and psychic ability (especially visions).

**Jade:** Healing, protection, wisdom, prosperity, love, longevity, fertility, and peace.

**Jasper:** Healing, protection, health, beauty, and energy.

**Jet:** Protection (especially from hexes). Alleviates fear.

**Kunzite:** Creativity, balance, communication, grounding, and relaxation.

**Kyanite:** Emotional balance.

**Lapiz lazuli:** Courage, creativity, joy, love, fidelity, protection, healing, beauty, and prosperity.

**Lepidolite:** Peace, spirituality, luck, protection, psychic ability, and emotional balance. Alleviates nightmares.

**Lodestone:** Cleansing.

**Malachite:** Power, energy, protection, love, peace, and success (especially in business and gardening).

**Marble:** Protection, dream recall, and meditation.

**Moldavite:** Psychic ability and emotional balance.

**Moonstone:** Grounding, love, divination, relaxation (especially sleep), protection, harmony, peace, youthfulness, and fortune (especially in gardening and travel).

**Obsidian:** Grounding, divination, and protection. Alleviates negativity.

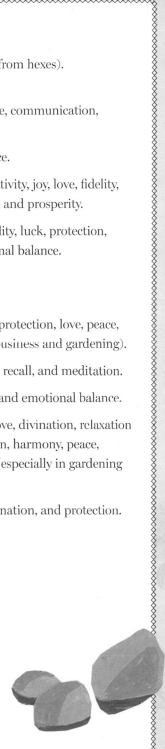

**Onyx:** Emotional balance, self-control, binding, protection, and strength.

**Opal:** Beauty, prosperity, luck, power, psychic abilities, and emotional balance.

**Pearl:** Peace, serenity, and truthfulness.

**Peridot:** Protection, prosperity, relaxation (especially sleep), health, emotional balance, and intuition.

**Rhodochrosite:** Energy, peace, calm, love, and emotional balance.

**Rose quartz:** Love, peace, happiness, and healing.

**Ruby:** Prosperity, power, courage, integrity, and joy. Alleviates nightmares.

**Rutilated quartz:** Communication.

**Sapphire:** Psychic abilities, inspiration, love, meditation, peace, healing, power, prosperity, and protection.

**Smokey quartz:** Healing and transformation. Alleviates negative energy.

**Sodalite:** Healing, meditation, wisdom, calm, grounding. Alleviates stress.

**Sugilite:** Love and harmony. Alleviates negative energy.

**Sunstone:** Protection, energy, health, passion, and sexuality.

**Tektite:** Enhancement (especially of energy) and enlightenment.

**Tiger's eye:** Courage, prosperity, protection, energy, luck, judgment and common sense, honesty, and divination. Alleviates depression.

**Topaz:** Protection, healing, prosperity, love, emotional balance, tranquility, and creativity.

**Tourmaline:** Love, friendship, prosperity, business, peace, relaxation (especially sleep), energy, courage, protection, and inspiration.

**Turquoise:** Courage, protection, prosperity, luck, friendship, healing, communication, happiness, emotional balance, and astral travel.

**Unakite:** Power and transformation (especially negative energy into positive energy).

**Zircon:** Protection, beauty, love, peace, sexual energy, healing, alertness, and emotional balance.

# Animals

We all have a sacred, "totem" animal. I was surprised to learn that mine is a deer, which I discovered when a young doe walked alongside me for two amazing hours. Tap into the power of animals by integrating animal symbolism—or even the animals themselves—into your magical ceremonies. Record the results in your Book of Shadows to reveal which creatures have the most powerful influence on your rituals and ceremonies—and perhaps even discover your own totem animal along the way.

**Bird:** Travel, mental ability (especially memory), and divination.

**Canary:** Harmony, joy, love, and luck.

**Chameleon:** Mutability, invisibility, protection, and power over the weather.

**Cat:** Independence, protection, uncovering secrets, and communication with spirits.

**Dog:** Loyalty, sustained effort, hearing, friendship, and protection.

**Fish:** Wealth, family, children, divination, and attraction (especially love).

**Frog:** Initiation, transformation, and regeneration. Alleviates negative energy and psychic blocks.

**Lizard:** Dreams (divination) and imagination.

**Lovebirds:** Love (especially marriage, partnership, and companionship).

**Parrot:** Impersonation and repetition.

**Snakes:** Creativity, wisdom, psychic ability, rebirth and regeneration, and communication with spirits.

**Spider:** Insight, originality, and new beginnings.

**Turtle:** Patience, perspicacity, and longevity.

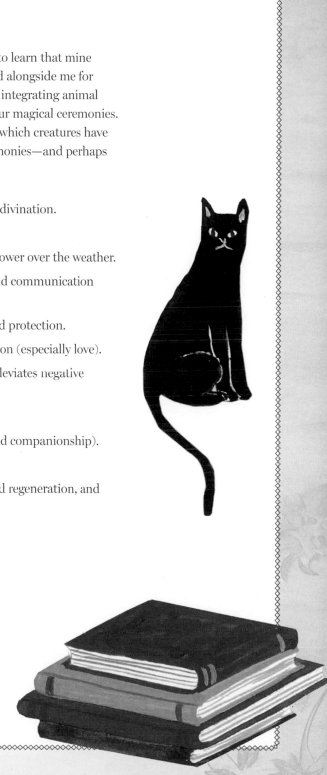

# Numbers and Their Magical Powers

Numerology is a magical discipline devised millennia ago—the earliest known system was developed by Pythagoras, a Greek philosopher from the 6th century BCE. The Pythagoreans, followers of Pythagoras, invested specific numbers with mystical properties and related them to heavenly bodies such as the Sun, Moon, and the planets. The correspondences listed opposite are based on the ancient Pythagorean system (on which modern-day numerology is founded).

The number three is of special significance to Wiccans, because of the three-by-three law (whatever you send out will be returned to you threefold). In numerology it is also linked to the three-fold nature of divinity, or the Trinity, and to the connection between mind, body, and spirit. The number four invokes the four elements of Earth, Air, Fire, and Water and the four directions of North, East, South, and West. The number seven is significant due to the seven chakras of the body and seven heavens, while eight signifies infinity.

With careful notes in your Book of Shadows, you will quickly find out which are your lucky numbers and, if a number keeps appearing to you in various forms, pay attention to its meaning because this will have a bearing on your daily life and magical workings.

## MASTER NUMBERS

In the Pythagorean tradition, master numbers were thought to have a special power and significance of their own. Eleven is linked to intuition, clairvoyance, and spiritual healing. Twenty-two is connected to the unlimited potential of mastery in any area (spiritual, physical, emotional, and mental). Finally, thirty-three indicates that all things are possible.

**One:** Independence, individuality, new beginnings, self-development, progress, and creativity.

**Two:** Balance (especially of yin and yang energies), selflessness and dedication (especially to others), attraction (especially between two people), and compromise.

**Three:** Expansion, expression, communication, fun, self-expression, giving outwardly, openness, and optimism.

**Four:** Security, foundations, self-discipline (especially of work and service), productivity, organization, and wholeness.

**Five:** Freedom, action and energy (especially physical), transformation, adventure, resourcefulness, travel, curiosity, impulsiveness, and excitement.

**Six:** Self-harmony, compassion, love, service (especially to the community), social responsibility, beauty, the arts, generosity, concern, caring, children, and balance.

**Seven:** Inner life and inner wisdom, birth and rebirth, strength (especially religious), commitment, solitude, analysis, and contemplation.

**Eight:** Prosperity, power, abundance, cosmic consciousness, reward, authority, and leadership.

**Nine:** Humanitarianism, selflessness and dedication (especially to others), completion, endings, compassion, tolerance, and wisdom.

# The Planets

Before the time of telescopes, the Ancient Greeks could see five planets in the night's sky (Mercury, Venus, Mars, Jupiter, and Saturn) as well as the Sun and Moon. They thought of each planet as a deity and understood their cosmic connection with those of us on Earth. Modern astrologers have since identified Uranus, Neptune, and Pluto, and today we can also recognize their divine influence on human affairs. Align your magical intentions with the influence of the planets and their associated deities to boost your spellwork and invoke the power of the gods.

**The Sun (Sol):** Family, gatherings, luck, success, and exorcism.

**Mercury (Mercury or Hermes):** Communication, travel, wisdom, and intelligence.

**Venus (Venus or Aphrodite):** Love, sex, peace, joy, happiness, friendship, and beauty.

**Moon (Luna or Diana):** Emotions, spirituality, sleep, psychism and divination, and fertility.

**Mars (Mars or Ares):** Power, courage, new beginnings, healing and health, and protection.

**Jupiter (Jupiter or Thor):** Employment, money, and wealth.

**Saturn (Saturn or Cronus):** Work, long-term plans, home, and banishing.

**Uranus (Uranus or Caelus):** Freedom, originality, and transformation (especially sudden change).

**Neptune (Neptune or Poseidon):** Dreams, illusions, and psychic ability. Alleviates uncertainty.

**Pluto (Pluto or Hades):** Wealth and prosperity (especially harvest), and the subconscious.

# PLANETARY COLOR

The ancient Sumerians and Chaldeans (see page 88) amassed enormous knowledge about the movement of the stars and planets. For example, the Dog Star, properly referred to as Sirius A, and its mate, Sirius B, was sacred and often celebrated with feasts. They knew the densities of the stars and the length of their orbit (fifty years), and since Sirius A was the brightest star in the night sky, they connected it to the beautiful blue stone they considered to be both powerful and precious: lapis lazuli. They devised a color coding for the stars and planets as the basis for their astrological system. When invoking the deities for help with your magical workings, incorporating these colors into your magical correspondences can boost the power of your spells enormously.

**The Sun:** Yellow.

**Mercury:** Blue.

**Venus:** Green.

**Moon:** White.

**Mars:** Rose, pink, and red.

**Jupiter:** Light blue.

**Saturn:** Purple.

**Uranus:** Violet.

**Neptune:** Aquamarine and green.

**Pluto:** Black.

# Metals and Magical Correspondences

Metals hold energies of tremendous influence and power. Witchcraft has long incorporated the use of metals in magic but, as alchemists have become few and far between, it has become more rarified. Today, metallurgy plays a definitive role in the enchantment of metal in jewelry and postmodern Pagans make the most direct connection with the power of metal through protection pieces such as amulets and talismans.

**Gold:** Faith (especially religious), protection (especially against harm or illness), confidence and courage, positivity, self-esteem, and wealth.

**Silver:** Communication, healing, mental ability (especially quick thinking), magical ability (especially lunar), amplification (especially self-esteem), and love.

**Copper:** Attraction (especially love), confidence, freedom, purification, self-esteem, luck, and healing. Alleviates sickness and lethargy.

**Brass:** Wealth, healing, protection, and purification. Alleviates hair loss.

**Bronze:** Healing, strength (especially of character), divination (especially scrying), focus, and success.

## MYSTICAL METALS

Many metals can enhance the power of any gem or crystal with "quickening" energy (a magical boost). Combine these precious metals with gems, sacred stones, and crystals (see magical correspondences on pages 128–130) for beautiful jewelry that is charged with magical power.

Lapis, jade, emeralds, and pearls attract love when set in silver.

Copper attracts love, especially if set with emerald, and you can boost its lucky power by wearing it with crystals of tiger's eye, coral, opal, or Apache tear. The healing energy of copper works well with stones such as azurite, chrysocolla, malachite, and turquoise, which already contain a trace of copper ore. Tiger's eye, aventurine, rhodonite, and mica are other metal-rich stones that combine their healing energy beautifully with copper.

Brass offers healing and protection, especially if shaped into a dog-, falcon-, or snake-shaped brooch.

# Deities and Their Domains

The lore of gods and goddesses and the power and associations therein are immensely valuable information to have in your Book of Shadows. The more information you have, the more you can access and work with these deities. Below is a list of international gods and goddesses through the ages and their related domains. By keeping track of your work with deities, you may be very surprised at which of these immortals abet your magic.

**Creativity:** Apollo, Athena, Benten, Bragi, Brigid, Ea, Hathor, Odin, Orpheus, Thor, Thoth, Untunktahe, Woden, and Xolotl.

**Communication:** Hermes, Janus, and Mercury.

**Courage:** Tyr.

**Fertility and childbirth:** Althea, Amnu, Anaitis, Anahita, Apollo, Arrianrhod, Asherali, Astarte, Attis, Baal, Bacchus, Bast, Bes, Bona Dea, Boucca, Camenta, Centeotle, Cernunnos, Cerridwen, Cihualtcoatl, Cuchavira, Cybele, Daghda, Demeter, Dew, Dionysus, Eostre, Frey, Freya, Frigg, Indra, Ishtar, Ishwara, Isis, Kronos, Kuan Yin, Ono, Laima, Lucina, Lulpercus, Meshkent, Min, Mut, Mylitta, Ningirsu, Ops, Osiris, Ostara, Pan, Pomona, Quetzalcoatl, Rhea, Rhiannon, Saturn, Selkhet, Sida, Tane, Telepinu, Telluno, Tellus Mater, Thunor, Tlazolteotl, Yarilo, and Zarpanitu.

**Good luck and fortune:** Bonus Eventus, Daikoku, Fortuna, Ganesa, Jorojin, Laima, and Tyche.

**Healing:** Apollo, Asclepius, Bast, Brigid, Eir, Gula, Ixlilton, Khnos, and Paeon.

**Journeys:** Echua and Janus.

**Justice and truth:** Astraea, Maat, Misharu, and Themis.

**Love and marriage:** Airyaman, Aizen, Alpan, Angus, Aphrodite, Aryan, Asera, Astarte, Asthoreth, Bah, Belili, Bes, Ceres, Creirwy, Cupid, Dzydzilelya, Eros, Errata, Erzulie, Esmeralda, Fenrua, Freya, Frigg, Habondia, Hathor, Hera, Hymen, Inanna, Ishtar, Juno, Kades, Kama, Kivan-Non, Kubaba, Melusine, Menu, Minnc, Mamaja, Odudua, Olwen, Oshun, Patina, Prenda, Rao, Saluki, Sauska, Svarog, Thalassa, Tlazoletotl, Turan, Tutunis, Venus, Vor, Xochipilli, and Zochiquetzal.

**Sleep and dreams:** Geshtinanna, Hypnos, Morpheus, and Nanshe.

**Wisdom:** Aruna, Athena, Atri, Baldur, Brigid, Dainichi, Ea, Enki, Fudo-Myoo, Fugen Bosatsu, Fukurokuju, Ganesha, Minerva, Nebo, Mimir, Oannes, Odin, Oghama, Quetzalxoatl, Sia, Sin, Thoth, Vohumano, and Zeus.

# Conclusion

Your Book of Shadows is your personal and private record of spells, rituals, notes, and observations of your witchcraft.

It will become an invaluable tool and an essential resource in the study of magic: in it, you'll record important spells and rituals you create or discover.

Like you, your Book of Shadows is
unique. Because you are an utterly
distinctive being, it may well be that
you didn't want to buy a Book of
Shadows off the shelf. In the early pages of this book,
we have explored how to bring your special energy to
choosing and creating your own sacred tome, from embellishing
and adorning your book in such a way that it reflects you and
represents your true essence (see pages 24–27) to channeling your creativity
with confidence (see pages 28–29). Your Book of Shadows is worth protecting;
your spellcraft is deeply personal and should remain so, with the exceptions
of what you want to share with your tribe. There is plenty of advice on this on
pages 30–35. As you know from the early chapters herein, to get the most use and
enjoyment of your Book of Shadows you will need to set positive intentions, create
a shrine or sacred space for your book, and include the laws of your tradition (the
core rules you and your coven follow) along with your sacred text, recipes, records
of your spells, and the magical correspondences that work best for you.

As your make your way through the lunar cycles, the astrological phases, and the
Pagan year, you will make adjustments to your spellwork, from tiny tweaks to major
changes. That is exactly what your Book of Shadows is for—to track your magic and
make improvements along the way. Your Book of Shadows is a diary of your magic.
When you create a ritual, perform a spell, or plant herb seeds under the light of the
right moon, you should log it in your Book of Shadows. You can and should look
back later and see how you're progressing along your witchy journey.

While the Book of Shadows basics are covered in this tome, I know your
creativity runs rich and deep. The only limit to what you can achieve with your
Book of Shadows is your imagination. In other words, no limit at all! Take time
to curate a Book of Shadows that is truly reflective of you. After all, you will be
spending a great deal of time with this book; make it a tool you love.

# Resources

## The Sabbats

Samhain (Hallows): October 31

Yule (winter solstice): December 2

Imbolc: February 1

Ostara (spring equinox): March 21

Beltane: May 1

Litha (summer solstice): June 21

Lughnasadh: August 2

Mabon (autumn equinox): September 22

## Almanacs

**The Old Farmer's Almanac**
www.almanac.com/topics/astronomy/moon/
moon-phase
*For phases of the moon, sun and moon signs,
gardening advice, recipes, and projects for home
and garden (also available in print).*

**The Witches' Almanac**
http://thewitchesalmanac.com
*For lunar lore, herbal lore, and astrological
information.*

## Crystals, Oils, Herbs, and Other Supplies

**Crystals by Nature**
https://crystalsbynature.nl
*For crystals, Tibetan rock salt, fossils, gems,
and jewelry.*

**Crystal Age**
www.crystalage.com
*For crystals, wands, crystalline statuary, and jewelry.*

**Fossilera**
www.fossilera.com
*For petrified wood and fossils.*

**Juniper Tree Supplies**
http://junipertreesupplies.com
*For essential oils, carrier oils, soap,
and candle-making supplies.*

**Herbs & Arts**
www.herbsandarts.com
*For incense, burners, supplies, and herbs.*

**The Scarlet Sage Herb Co.**
www.scarletsage.com
*For dried herbs, essential oils, floral waters, and books.*

**Trader Joe's**
www.traderjoes.com
*For mini brooms.*

# Gardening

**Savvy Gardening**
www.savvygardening.com
*For gardening instructions and information
on zones and climate.*

**Gardener's Supply Company**
www.gardeners.com
*For supplies.*

**General Gardening Resources**
www.gardeningchannel.com/gardening-resources-
best-gardening-sites
www.thegardeningwebsite.co.uk
www.rhs.org.uk

# Astrology

**Cafe Astrology**
www.cafeastrology.com
*Hugely useful site for all your astrology needs.
Use the following links when working out your
lunar birthday:*

*To find out your sun sign:*
www.cafeastrology.com/whats-my-sun-sign.html

*To find out your moon sign:*
www.cafeastrology.com/whats-my-moon-sign.html

*To find the ephemeris for previous and upcoming years
to determine your lunar birthday:*
www.cafeastrology.com/ephemeris.html

# Index

# Acknowledgments

This book is a long-held dream come true. For many years, I have wanted to share some of my discoveries about tracking magic and using a Book of Shadows to evolve and abet spiritual growth. I am very blessed to have the opportunity to do so with the marvelous team of CICO Books and I owe huge gratitude to my editor Kristine Pidkameny and her colleagues, Kristy Richardson and Carmel Edmonds, a triple goddess trio of excellence in all things editorial. Every book CICO makes is a work of art with such close attention to design, illustrations, and the craft of making beautiful books. My dream Book of Shadows is in very good hands with designer, Emily Breen, and illustrator, Iratxe Lopez de Munain. Great gratitude to the highly skilled and caring team. Brava!

# Picture Credits

All illustrations by Iratxe López de Munáin, except the following:
Bárbara Tamilin: pages 96 (bottom) and 97 © CICO Books; Julia Cellini: pages 50 (top left), 52 (top left), 56 (top left), and 60 (top left) © Julia Cellini. © Adobestock.com: paranoic_fb: background illustrations on pages 1, 4–13, 16–19, 22–59, 64–79, 82–109, 112–144; Kseniia Velledynska: background illustrations on pages 2–3, 14–15, 20–21, 60–63, 72–73, 80–81, 110–111; Christos Georghiou: background illustration on pages 6, 90, 93; Samiramay: page 11; Pixejoo: pages 31 (right), 91 (right), 93 (right), 99; netsign: page 70.